NEXT-GENERATION
MEDICAL TECHNOLOGY

Nanotechnology and Medicine

Don Nardo

ReferencePoint
Press®

San Diego, CA

© 2018 ReferencePoint Press, Inc.
Printed in the United States

For more information, contact:
ReferencePoint Press, Inc.
PO Box 27779
San Diego, CA 92198
www.ReferencePointPress.com

LIBRARY OF CONGRESS CATALOGING-IN-PUBLICATION DATA

Name: Nardo, Don, 1947– author.
Title: Nanotechnology and Medicine/by Don Nardo.
Description: San Diego, CA: ReferencePoint Press, Inc., 2018. | Series:
   Next-Generation Medical Technology series | Audience: Grade 9 to 12. |
   Includes bibliographical references and index.
Identifiers: LCCN 2017035665 (print) | LCCN 2017044344 (ebook) | ISBN
   9781682823286 (eBook) | ISBN 9781682823279 (hardback)
Subjects: LCSH: Nanomedicine—Juvenile literature. | Nanotechnology—Juvenile
   literature. | Medical innovations—Juvenile literature.
Classification: LCC R857.N34 (ebook) | LCC R857.N34 N37745 2018 (print) | DDC
   610.28—dc23
LC record available at https://lccn.loc.gov/2017035665

CONTENTS

IMPORTANT EVENTS IN THE HISTORY OF NANOTECHNOLOGY

1959
American physicist Richard Feynman gives a groundbreaking lecture in which he describes nanoparticles and predicts some of their future uses.

1897
British scientist J.J. Thomson discovers the first-known subatomic particle—the electron.

| 1800 | / | 1920 | 1950 | 1980 |

1911
British physicist Ernest Rutherford describes the atom's core, including the protons and neutrons within it.

1974
Tokyo University of Science professor Norio Taniguchi coins the term *nanotechnology*.

1803
English chemist John Dalton advances the first modern theory of atoms; their domain will later come to be called the nano realm of matter.

1981
IBM scientists Gerd Binnig and Heinrich Rohrer invent the scanning tunneling microscope (STM), which allows humans to directly image atoms and the nano realm for the first time.

1985
Scientists at Rice University in Houston, Texas, discover carbon nanoparticles called fullerenes, which they nickname buckyballs.

1989
Using the STM, IBM physicist Don Eigler moves thirty-five xenon atoms so that they form the letters IBM.

2013
Scientists at the University of Basel in Switzerland begin work on an efficient contrast agent made of nanoparticles for use in magnetic resonance imaging machines.

2012
The National Aeronautics and Space Administration announces its creation of the biocapsule, a drug delivery system constructed of carbon nanotubes.

| 1985 | 1995 | 2005 | 2015 | 2025 |

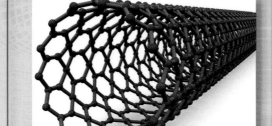

2017
Researchers at the University of Notre Dame in Indiana announce that they have used nanotechnology to develop a method for early diagnosis of peanut allergy.

1991
Japanese scientist Sumio Iijima discovers an important fullerene cousin, the nanotube, or buckytube.

1986
American engineer K. Eric Drexler publishes *Engines of Creation: The Coming Era of Nanotechnology*, a book that introduces the concept of nanotechnology to the general public.

2014
IBM announces it will replace its traditional silicon computer transistors with nanotech versions by 2020.

The Incredibly Tiny Nano Realm

In a laboratory at the Imperial College London in 2012, noted infectious diseases expert Sunil Shaunak experienced what all scientists long for—the thrill of a new and important discovery. He and his research team had long been trying to find a cure for a kind of infection that kills more than 100 million people each year worldwide. Called shigellosis, it is caused by a bacterium, or germ, called *shigella*.

This scourge causes severe, life-threatening diarrhea. Even worse, the germs cause the victim's immune system to overreact. It sends powerful chemicals to fight the invaders. The ensuing explosive microscopic battle, called septic shock, causes the intestinal walls to rupture. The sinister *shigella* infection then spreads into the body cavity, leading to a painful death. "It's a catastrophe that unfolds in front of your eyes," Shaunak says. "We do a good job of killing the bug but we do nothing to control the excessive immune response of the patient."[1]

When he had begun his infection-related research ten years before, Shaunak had hoped to learn how to stop the *shigella* microbe from killing people. He recalls that he knew "doctors have a powerful arsenal of antibiotics, antivirals and antifungals at their disposal." All had been tried, yet none had worked very well against shigellosis. "Patients were still dying."[2]

Fooling the Germs

So Shaunak decided to try something new and untested in this area of research. He turned to the growing scientific discipline of nanotechnology. This field deals with the incredibly tiny realm in which objects are measured in nanometers. A nanometer equals one billionth of a meter, or about one three-hundred-millionth of a foot. To get an idea of how small that is, consider that an average bacterium, like a *shigella* germ, measures about one thousand to five thousand nanometers in diameter. Then consider that hundreds of thousands of bacteria that size can fit inside the period at the end of a sentence.

dendrimer

a kind of nanoparticle, or artificial molecule, that features branching structures, making it resemble a tiny tree

Working in the nano realm, Shaunak reasoned, might allow him to manipulate the immune system in favor of the person suffering from the serious infection. Evidence showed that the body's immune cells are attracted to specific structures that are located on the outer surfaces of the bacteria. Shaunak theorized that he might be able to fashion tiny structures that would mimic the real ones but not trigger septic shock.

The researchers focused on nanoparticles known as dendrimers. They are molecules—made up of a wide variety of combinations of atoms—that have already shown promise in carrying medicines directly to human cells. Shaunak and his team engineered the dendrimers so that they would coat the germs' surfaces and hopefully attract the body's immune cells. Then they tested the idea on rabbits that they had infected with shigellosis.

Sure enough, the rabbits' immune cells detected and targeted the dendrimers coating the bacteria. But the interaction that followed had a fairly mild impact and did not lead to the dangerous outcome so often seen in cases of shigellosis. Little or no damage to the intestinal walls occurred, and most of the rabbits recovered. The excited Shaunak realized that his nanoparticles had—at least in a highly specific situation—acted very much like a powerful antibiotic. This suggested that perhaps sometime in the future certain engineered nanoparticles might even replace some antibiotics. "We are in new and uncharted waters when it comes to applying dendrimer-based-nanotechnology to infection[s],"[3] he stated.

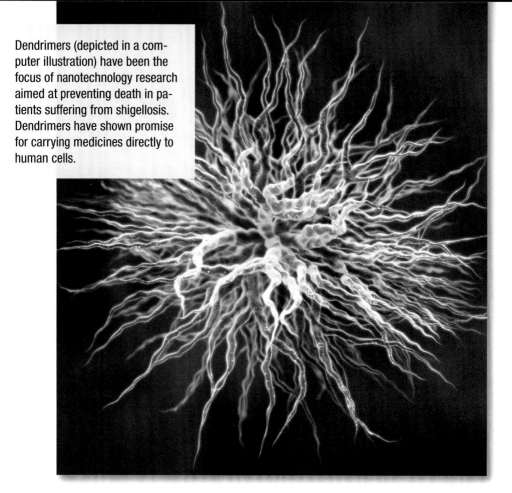

Dendrimers (depicted in a computer illustration) have been the focus of nanotechnology research aimed at preventing death in patients suffering from shigellosis. Dendrimers have shown promise for carrying medicines directly to human cells.

A Significant Impact on Society

Shaunak's highly specific research area is one of hundreds that are presently attempting to exploit the potential benefits of nanotechnology. Thousands of medical researchers and numerous other kinds of scientists around the world are experimenting with nanoparticles of various kinds. Meanwhile, some of these remarkable substances are already in use in hospitals, factories, computer labs, farms, and elsewhere.

Moreover, each year millions of people begin using products manufactured with the aid of nanotechnology. In fact, that growing field is increasingly having a "significant impact on almost all industries and all areas of society," states the Center for Responsible Nanotechnology, a nonprofit think tank in Tucson, Arizona. The center contends that in the future nanotechnology will continue to offer "better built, longer lasting, cleaner, safer, and smarter products for the home, for communications, for medicine, for transportation, for agriculture, and for industry in general."[4]

That view—that nanotechnology has nothing less than huge potential—is shared by the prestigious National Science Foundation. "Imagine," a foundation spokesperson says, "a medical device that travels through the human body to seek out and destroy small clusters of cancerous cells before they can spread. Or a box no larger than a sugar cube that contains the entire contents of the Library of Congress. Or materials much lighter than steel that possess ten times as much strength."[5]

Thousands of applications for nanotechnology in a wide variety of fields either exist or are in development. Only a few include miniature electronic circuits for a wide variety of machines, advanced explosives detectors, agricultural methods and food production, substances that prevent rust, effective ways to clean up oil spills, very tiny microchips for smaller and smaller computers, more efficient golf and tennis balls, and new kinds of sunscreens, cosmetics, paints, varnishes, and car fuels.

Benefiting All of Humankind

In particular, medical applications, including the device that seeks and destroys cancer cells, are increasing by the hundreds each year. "Nanotechnology medical developments over the coming years will have a wide variety of uses," states Eleonore Pauwels of the Wilson Center for scholarly research in Washington, DC. That new scientific tool, she says, "could potentially save a great number of lives."[6]

Doctors in hospitals are already using that tool to help diagnose various illnesses. They are also employing nanotechnology to deliver various kinds of medicine to targeted areas of the body. In addition, medical technicians are using nanotechnology principles to manufacture artificial skin to replace damaged skin tissue.

Meanwhile, in labs worldwide major research is being conducted into manipulating DNA, the microscopic blueprint of human life. The goal is to successfully treat and eventually cure maladies such as diabetes, AIDS, cancer, and cystic fibrosis. These are only a few examples of how nanotechnology has "the potential to benefit all of humankind," say scientists Linda Williams and Wade Adams. "Imagination and function are becoming reality. Today we are fast approaching a chance to touch the future in ways that haven't made this much difference since iron (versus bronze) was the hot topic around the campfire."[7]

CHAPTER 1

The Origins of Nanotechnology

Noted physicist and futurist Michio Kaku has been observing and commenting on the unfolding nanotechnology revolution for more than three decades. He keeps track of the many advances the new technology is making in medicine, manufacturing, agriculture, and numerous other areas. Part of his job as a futurist is to project these advances forward and predict where they will lead in the decades and centuries ahead.

Kaku foresees that possibly as early as 2070 scientists will achieve one of the ultimate goals of nanotechnology—and of science in general—which is the development of a replicator. He describes a replicator as a device perhaps the size of a washing machine that will be capable of creating virtually any product from basic raw materials. The key to this ability he says, will be nanobots—robot-like assemblers that will exist and do their jobs on the incredibly tiny scale of atoms and molecules. A person will put some raw materials into the replicator, Kaku explains. "Trillions upon trillions of nanobots would then converge on the raw materials," he continues. Each nanobot will be

> programmed to take them apart molecule by molecule and then reassemble them into an entirely new product. This machine would be able to manufacture anything. The replicator would be the crowning achievement of engineering and science, the ultimate culmination of our struggles ever since we picked up the first tool back in prehistory.[8]

Like that first human tool—perhaps a tree branch used as a club—Kaku points out, the nanobots that will inhabit the future replicator are tools as well. The essential difference is that they are far more advanced in concept and execution than the tools that humans fashioned in prior ages. As the best futurists always do, Kaku looks backward as well as forward. He realizes that the key to forecasting where a scientific discipline is heading is understanding where and when it originated and how it has gradually developed.

Room at the Bottom

Kaku and other modern scientists rather precisely pinpoint the beginning of the modern nanotechnology revolution to December 29, 1959. That was the day that celebrated physicist and college professor Richard Feynman gave a lecture that forever changed the world. The title of the talk, delivered at the California Institute of Technology, was "There's Plenty of Room at the Bottom." Its theme was the idea of human beings delving into and exploiting the extremely tiny "bottom" world of atoms and molecules. "What I want to talk about," he told his audience, "is the problem of manipulating and controlling things on a small scale."[9]

> **nanobot**
>
> an extremely tiny robot-like device that can assemble atoms and molecules into various substances and products

Granted, Feynman went on, people had already managed to achieve an impressive degree of miniaturization of certain tools and objects. There were, he said, electric motors "the size of the nail on your small finger." Also, there was a device available that could write the Lord's Prayer on the head of a pin. "But that's nothing!" Feynman asserted, surprising many of his listeners. "That's the most primitive, halting step in the direction I intend to discuss." Seeing numerous raised eyebrows in the hall, he pointedly asked, "Why cannot we write the entire 24 volumes of the *Encyclopedia Britannica* on the head of a pin?"[10]

Such a thing would be possible, Feynman said, if humans could somehow manipulate individual atoms and molecules using tremendously tiny and precise tools. Among those implements,

11

he suggested, would be microscopic robot-like devices with the equivalent of hands that could move and build with individual atoms and molecules. This would allow scientists to do all sorts of things that were either considered impossible or had yet to be conceived. "At the atomic level," he stated, "we have new kinds of forces and new kinds of possibilities, new kinds of effects." He added that he could foresee a future in which "chemical forces are used in a repetitious fashion to produce all kinds of weird effects."[11]

The Evolution of the Atomic Theory
Feynman's innovative concept of manipulating the microscopic world relied on the already existing knowledge of atoms and molecules. He often cited his debt to the earlier thinkers who had defined and described those minuscule elements that make up matter. Indeed, he recognized that the true origins of the new technology he proposed lay with the discoveries of those earlier researchers.

In his physics classes, Feynman described the evolution of the atomic theory and properly gave credit to Democritus and other ancient Greek scientists for being the first to propose that idea. Democritus had declared that all matter is composed of atoms—individual particles or building blocks too small to see. After the close of ancient times in the fifth and sixth centuries CE, the atomic concept was largely lost. But Western thinkers rediscovered it in early modern times.

English chemist John Dalton put forward the first modern theory of atoms in about 1803. He suggested that various natural substances and chemical reactions occur because atoms either come together or break apart. When they come together, he said, they form larger particles, which one of his contemporaries named molecules. Dalton assumed that an atom was the smallest existing particle of matter. This proved incorrect, however. A later British scientist, J.J. Thomson, discovered a subatomic (meaning "smaller than an atom") particle—the electron—in 1897.

At first Thomson and other researchers thought that an atom was composed only of electrons. But one of Thomson's pupils, physicist Ernest Rutherford, disagreed. In 1911 Rutherford concluded that an atom contains a central nucleus in which other subatomic particles—protons and neutrons—exist.

Nanoscale Measurements

Nanotechnology takes place at the submicroscopic level, meaning a world so small it cannot be seen even with a light microscope. The unit of measurement in nanotechnology, the nanometer, is one-billionth of a meter. This is much, much smaller than a centimeter, a millimeter, or a micrometer. In fact, a nanometer is about one hundred-thousandth the width of a single human hair. A comparison between the head of a pin, a single particle of ragweed pollen, a red blood cell, and a carbon nanotube (a tube-shaped carbon molecule that is much stronger than steel) illustrates the scale of nanotechnology.

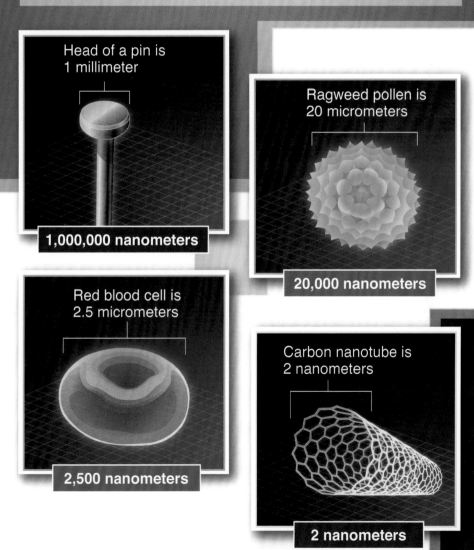

Head of a pin is 1 millimeter

1,000,000 nanometers

Ragweed pollen is 20 micrometers

20,000 nanometers

Red blood cell is 2.5 micrometers

2,500 nanometers

Carbon nanotube is 2 nanometers

2 nanometers

Subsequent studies of atoms and molecules demonstrated that the realm of these microscopic particles is fantastically tiny. In this world objects that people normally view as small are enormous. An often-cited example is a human hair, which to most people appears extremely thin. In the nano world, such a hair is seventy-five thousand nanometers in diameter.

In comparison, a hydrogen atom is about one-tenth of a nanometer wide. A more complex silicon atom is roughly one-fifth of a nanometer wide. Thus, one would have to line up 750,000 hydrogen atoms, or 375,000 silicon atoms, beside one another to equal the width of a human hair. Still another comparison that shows the tininess of the nano world uses marbles like those that children play with. If a nanoparticle that measures one nanometer wide was the size of a marble, an average person would be as tall as Mt. Everest—29,085 feet (8,848 m).

nanometer

a measurement that is one-billionth of a meter, or one three-hundred-millionth of a foot

The Essential Imaging Breakthrough

It was this astonishingly tiny nano world that Feynman had suggested might be manipulated in ways no one had considered before. Other scientists soon saw promise in that vision for the future. One was Norio Taniguchi, a professor at Tokyo University of Science in Japan. In 1974 he published a paper titled "On the Basic Concept of 'Nano-Technology.'" This was first time that anyone had ever used the term *nanotechnology*, and Taniguchi is still remembered for coining it.

In the paper, he further developed some of Feynman's ideas, saying that many unusual and useful substances might be created by using atoms and molecules in new ways. Yet to do so, Taniguchi said, would require new and better microscopes than currently existed. At the time, even the most powerful optical instruments were incapable of producing direct images of individual atoms.

The essential imaging breakthrough that Taniguchi spoke about came sooner than he had anticipated. Just seven years later, in 1981, Gerd Binnig and Heinrich Rohrer of IBM's research laboratory in Zurich, Switzerland, invented the scanning tunneling microscope (STM). For the first time, scientists could see atoms. Moreover, they could move some individual atoms from one place to another with the aid of a special pointed object. According to Kaku, the STM

resembles an old phonograph. A fine needle (with a tip that is only a single atom across) passes slowly over the material being analyzed. A small electrical current travels from the needle, through the material, to the base of the instrument. As the needle passes over the object, the electrical current changes slightly every time it passes over an atom. After multiple passes, the machine prints out the stunning outline of the atom itself. Using an identical needle [appropriately dubbed a nanoprobe], the microscope is then capable not just of recording these atoms, but also of moving them around.[12]

The Most Important Tool Ever Imagined

Many scientists have pointed out that nanotechnology represents the latest in a long series of increasingly sophisticated tools that humanity has created over the course of many centuries. City University of New York physics professor and noted futurist Michio Kaku explains, saying,

Throughout human history, the mastery of tools has determined our fate. When the bow and arrow were perfected thousands of years ago, it meant that we could fire projectiles much farther than our hands could throw them, increasing the efficiency of our hunting and increasing our food supply. When metallurgy was invented about 7,000 years ago, it meant that we could replace huts of mud and straw and eventually create great buildings that soared above the earth. Soon empires began to rise from the forest and the desert, built from the tools forged from metals. And now we are on the brink of mastering yet another type of tool, much more powerful than anything we have seen before. This time, we will be able to master the atoms themselves out of which everything is created. Within this century we may possess the most important tool ever imagined—nanotechnology that will allow us to manipulate individual atoms. This could begin a second industrial revolution, as molecular manufacturing creates new materials we can only dream about today, which are super-strong, super-light, with amazing electrical and magnetic properties.

Michio Kaku, *Physics of the Future*. New York: Doubleday, 2011, p. 173.

The most famous early demonstration of this direct manipulation of atoms was accomplished by IBM physicist Don Eigler in 1989. He used the STM at the IBM Almaden Research Center in San Jose, California, to move thirty-five atoms of the element xenon into the configuration he desired. That pattern spelled the letters *IBM*. "We wanted to show we could position atoms in a way that's very similar to how a child builds with Lego blocks," Eigler later recalled. "The ability to manipulate atoms, build structures of our own, [and] design and explore their functionality has changed people's outlook in many ways. It has been identified as one of the starting moments of nanotech because of the access it gave us to atoms."[13]

The Discovery of Buckyballs

After the introduction of the scanning tunneling microscope in 1981, the next major stride forward in nanotechnology took place in 1985 at Rice University in Houston, Texas. There, a team of chemists led by Richard Smalley, Harold Kroto, and Robert Curl

Chemist Harold Kroto poses with models of buckyballs, a new form of carbon that he and two other scientists discovered in 1985. Buckyballs, also called fullerenes, lie at the heart of the nanotechnology revolution.

made a remarkable discovery: a completely new form of the element carbon.

For a long time the main known types of complex carbon were graphite and diamond. Graphite is used widely in various industries and for making pencils, in which case it was long mistakenly called lead. According to Linda Williams and Wade Adams, "Graphite has a layered or planar (flat) structure. The carbon structure is complex, but mostly two-dimensional (2-D) in a flat plane—think chicken wire. Or you can think of graphite as being like a flat playing card."[14] The flat layers of graphite tend to slide over each other and under pressure can break up easily. This is why the graphite in pencils readily rubs off onto a piece of paper when someone writes with the pencil.

In contrast, diamond's structure is a three-dimensional lattice, often in the shape of a series of interconnected cubes. Each carbon atom in the lattice is attached by strong bonds to four other carbon atoms. The combination of the structure and bonds makes diamond the hardest and more durable of known naturally occurring substances.

fullerene

a large group of carbon atoms that are bound together in the shape of a geodesic dome

The discovery made by the Rice University team introduced a new form of carbon with a unique structure. It is sometimes called C_{60} because each molecule of it is composed of sixty carbon atoms. Such molecules are also frequently called fullerenes, or buckyballs. The last two names are homages to the late noted architect Richard Buckminster Fuller. He invented the famous geodesic dome, composed of multiple five-sided and six-sided flat surfaces that touch one another at angles and form a strong, rigid structure resembling a soccer ball. Fullerenes have a similar cage-like structure that gives them a combination of strength and flexibility.

The fullerene molecule is also very stable and can withstand high pressures and temperatures. For these and other reasons, scientists began to propose possible nanoscale applications for it, including body armor for soldiers and police and highly miniaturized electronic and computer parts. This huge potential of buckyballs made them the first major new substance related to the growing nanotechnology revolution. So significant was this new material that Smalley, Kroto, and Curl received the coveted Nobel Prize in Chemistry in 1996 for their earlier discovery of it.

Stronger Yet Lighter than Steel?

By that time the fullerene had company—a carbon cousin that came to be called the nanotube. Scientist Sumio Iijima of the NEC Fundamental Research Laboratories in Tsukuba, Japan, discovered the nanotube in 1991 while experimenting with fullerenes. Unlike the fullerene, which is shaped like a geodesic dome, the carbon nanotube, nicknamed the buckytube, is shaped like a cylinder. Images obtained from the STM reveal that the ends of the cylinders have rounded caps. Each cylinder contains many millions of carbon atoms.

nanotube

a large number of carbon atoms that are bound together in the shape of a cylinder

Scientists saw that nanotubes had other fascinating and promising properties. For example, their large numbers of carbon atoms can bond tightly with atoms in other kinds of substances they encounter. This makes them so tough that they can be made into fibers one hundred times stronger than steel yet have only one-sixth the weight of steel. Researchers reasoned that that quality might make nanotubes useful in various forms of construction. Another property that scientists observed was that one nanotube can slide within a slightly larger tube in a telescoping effect. This flexibility inspired applications that included lubricants, ball bearings, and tiny motors in microscopic machines.

One of the first concrete, direct applications of these newly discovered particles was a medical one, namely to kill bacteria that cause disease. A few years after the discovery of nanotubes, researchers led by chemist George John of the City College of New York managed to embed silver nanoparticles in paint. John knew that silver was known to be an effective antigerm agent. In the past, however, no one had broken silver down into particles smaller than one hundred nanometers in width in order to fight disease. John later explained that the "nanoparticles are very small and they are interacting with the bacteria and rupturing the [bacterial] cell wall."[15] If hospitals used such nanotube-laced paint on their walls, he said, it might well reduce cases of infection in those facilities.

Promises of Radical Abundance

Meanwhile, during this early period of research into fullerenes and nanotubes, a few experts sought to popularize the concept of nanotechnology by publishing reader-friendly books. One of these, by engineer and lecturer K. Eric Drexler, became a best-seller. First released in 1986 (and reprinted several times since), it bears the compelling title *Engines of Creation: The Coming Era of Nanotechnology*. In that work, Drexler builds directly on the concepts introduced in Feynman's seminal 1959 lecture. According to Drexler, in the near future scientists will create machines the size of a few molecules. These will feature tiny motors and robotic arms to grasp and maneuver individual atoms. Even entire computers will be miniaturized to microscopic size, he predicts,

Transistors (the blue pieces pictured on the right side of this integrated circuit board) are essential to the operation of computers. IBM hopes to eventually replace all traditional silicon transistors with ones made from carbon nanotubes.

perhaps to the size of a human cell or even smaller. The robotic assemblers will manufacture all manner of products, he goes on, all from raw materials such as rocks, trees, seawater, soil, and air: "Assemblers will be able to make virtually anything from common materials without labor, replacing smoking factories with systems as clean as forests. They will transform technology and the economy at their roots, opening a new world of possibilities. They will indeed be engines of abundance."[16]

Since *Engines of Creation* first appeared, scientists around the world have indeed begun to experiment with and implement nanotechnology in a wide variety of industrial, agricultural, and medical areas. One of the most impressive applications has been in the always advancing realm of computers. In 1998, for instance, IBM made a working carbon nanotube transistor. Tran-

The Coming of Nanotube Transistors

Tom Simonite, editor of the *MIT Technology Review*, provides this brief overview of IBM's present efforts to revolutionize computers using carbon nanotubes.

A project at IBM is now aiming to have transistors built using carbon nanotubes ready to take over from silicon transistors soon after 2020. According to the semiconductor industry's roadmap, transistors at that point must have features as small as five nanometers to keep up with the continuous miniaturization of computer chips. [In] 1998, researchers at IBM made one of the first working carbon nanotube transistors. And now, after more than a decade of research, IBM is the first major company to commit to getting the technology ready for commercialization. [The] target for commercialization [is] based on the timetable of technical improvements the chip industry has mapped out to keep alive Moore's Law, a prediction originating in 1965. [It stated] that the number of transistors that could be crammed into a circuit would double every two years. Generations of chip-making technology are known by the size of the smallest structure they can write into a chip. The current best is 14 nanometers, and by 2020, in order to keep up with Moore's Law, the industry will need to be down to five nanometers. This is the point IBM hopes nanotubes can step in. The most recent report from the microchip industry group the ITRS says the so-called five-nanometer "node" is due in 2019.

Tom Simonite, "IBM: Commercial Nanotube Transistors Are Coming Soon," *MIT Technology Review*, July 1, 2014. www.technologyreview.com.

sistors, which are essential to computer operation, are devices that switch or strengthen electronic signals.

This gadget was not then sophisticated enough to be used commercially in millions of computers. But over the years the company continued experimenting with nanotubes and made steady advances. In 2014 IBM announced that it hoped to replace all of its traditional silicon transistors with carbon nanotube transistors soon after 2020. This decision was largely based on the fact that the nanotube transistors are much smaller than the silicon ones. This will allow the computers to pack a lot more information and calculating capability into a smaller space, making the machines more powerful than those available today.

Such advances, Drexler said in one of his later books, are rapidly altering human technology. "Looking forward," he states, "we can see a molecular, mechanical, nanoscale technology that promises to change the material world as thoroughly as digital technologies have changed the world of information." First, he went on, there were the agricultural, industrial, and information revolutions. Nanotechnology, he foretells, will lie at the heart of the next major change: "It seems that our future holds a comparable technology-driven transformation, enabled by nanoscale devices, but this time with atoms in place of bits. The revolution that follows can bring a radical abundance beyond the dreams of any king, a post-industrial material abundance that reaches the ends of the Earth and lightens its burden."[17]

CHAPTER 2

Nanotechnology and Medical Diagnosis

Of the many scientific fields in which nanotechnology is making an increasingly large impact, one of the most prominent is medicine. "We think there's a strong promise for nanotechnology that's used in medicine," says Thomas Webster, chairman of the Department of Chemical Engineering at Northeastern University in Boston. As in other scientific areas, nanotechnology's exploitation of the ultramicroscopic world is what makes it particularly attractive for medical uses, he points out. "The small size" of various kinds of nanoparticles "allows you to penetrate cells, get inside cells and manipulate their function in ways that you can't do with conventional material."[18]

Within the broad and varied spectrum of the medical world, diagnosis is an area that has shown a good deal of promise when paired with nanotechnology. Diagnosis consists of detecting and identifying diseases and other illnesses. A number of fairly effective diagnostic techniques presently exist, yet all doctors concur that it would be better if they produced results faster. "A vital goal of diagnostic medicine," Webster explains, "is to be able to diagnose medical problems as swiftly as possible, enabling clinicians [doctors] to treat patients before any irreversible or long-lasting damage can occur." He continues,

> One problem that arises with diagnosing medical conditions is that the symptoms of some conditions only arise after a certain amount of time. By the time these symptoms come to the surface, the underlying condition will have progressed to a stage at which its treatment is much

more complicated than it would have been had the problem been discovered earlier. [This] problem is a common one.[19]

In recent years, increasing numbers of medical researchers have concluded that using nanoparticles of various kinds can often speed up the diagnosis process. As one researcher says, "Because of their small size, nanomaterials can readily interact with biomolecules,"[20] the molecules making up living tissue. That makes nanoparticles very useful in diagnosis. It allows doctors to detect disease symptoms in a small lab sample earlier than was possible in the past.

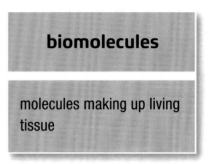

biomolecules

molecules making up living tissue

Moreover, nanomaterials offer doctors the ability to view interactions within cells in real time and during an illness's earliest stages.

Creating the Nanoparticles

As a result of these advantages, nanoparticles are already in limited use for diagnosis in medical labs around the world. Before using the nanoparticles this way, however, and in other medical ways as well, those tiny units of matter must first be created. Specially trained technicians employ two primary methods: the so-called top-down and bottom-up processes. Here, *top-down* refers to the mechanical crushing of a material, often a metal or a compound such as a metal oxide. (A metal oxide is a metal whose atoms have oxygen atoms attached to them.) Ceramic substances, which are composed of clay, silicon, and other nonmetallic materials, are also used in making nanoparticles in the top-down process.

These substances are pulverized in mills equipped with grinders made of steel. A mechanical assembly within the machine drives the grinder into the metal or ceramic sample with a great deal of energy. This converts the sample into very small pieces. As the grinder smashes into those particles again and again, they break up even more until finally some of them measure less than one hundred nanometers across. By definition, that makes them nanoparticles.

In the bottom-up method, by contrast, technicians use chemicals of various kinds to cause atoms to organize into the desired particles. The process works especially well with carbon atoms and is a common source of fullerenes and other carbon nanoparticles. A traditional carbon source, such as graphite or soot, is exposed to a special vapor produced by an arc of electricity or a laser. The vapor induces many of the carbon atoms in the source to reorganize into nanoparticles such as carbon nanotubes.

More Effective Contrast Agents

One of the newest diagnostic uses for nanoparticles is to produce more effective imaging of body parts. In medical imaging, doctors look inside the body using several traditional methods. These include taking a tissue sample and examining it under a microscope; taking an X-ray of one or more body parts; subject-

A doctor talks with her patient about an X-ray. Nanomaterials, which work at the cellular level, might enable doctors to diagnose illnesses at much earlier stages than they can with traditional tools such as X-rays.

ing parts of the body to an MRI (magnetic resonance imaging) machine, which employs a powerful magnet to produce images; and ultrasound, which makes an image by passing sound waves through the body. In X-rays, MRIs, and ultrasounds, often unhealthy tissues are hard to see because there is not enough contrast between them and healthy tissues. To overcome this obstacle, doctors have learned to inject so-called contrast agents into the bloodstream. When such an agent reaches the target site, it increases the contrast and thereby makes the image clearer and easier to read and interpret.

Traditional chemical contrast agents have their limitations, however. For instance, often they do not penetrate all the way into tissues, making sections of those tissues hard to image in MRI machines. With this in mind, in recent years medical researchers began using nanoparticles as contrast agents. Because they are so tiny, the nanoparticles can penetrate the tissue more thoroughly than the traditional agents. Also, some metal nanoparticles have magnetic properties, which make them excellent candidates for use in an MRI machine.

Between 2013 and 2016, Severin I. Sigg and other scientists at the University of Basel in Switzerland developed an efficient contrast agent made of nanoparticles for use in MRIs. According to a university spokesperson, the "new type of nanoparticles produces around ten times more contrast than [traditional] contrast agents."[21] The new technology is being tested on animals and will likely see wide use as a diagnostic tool for humans as early as 2020.

Nanoparticles Pinpoint Infections

In addition to enhancing imaging methods, nanoparticles can identify all sorts of medical problems. One of the most common of all such problems is an infection, along with the inflammation that can accompany it. One of the biggest difficulties doctors have in diagnosing infections is that these maladies always start on a small—in fact, microscopic—scale. An infection can be well developed and feature the buildup of many millions of bacteria before a hospital lab can identify it.

Webster and his team have studied this problem in relation to infections that sometimes form in newly inserted hip joint implants. If some bacteria find their way into the implant, he points out, it can become infected or inflamed. In many cases, he adds, "by the time it becomes apparent that a hip implant has become infected, [the] only solution is to remove the implant and insert a new one."[22]

The solution that Webster and his colleagues came up with is to use nanoparticles to more easily and more rapidly diagnose an infection. The particles work well for two reasons. First, they are so small that they can penetrate the multiple layers of an infection. As Webster says, in some bacterial infections the germs grow in slimy layers, usually called biofilms. "We've been able to develop these nanoparticles that can actually penetrate those biofilms,"[23] Webster reports. That gives a doctor the potential to find and diagnose an infection while it is still small and difficult to locate using traditional methods.

biofilm

a slimy layer of bacteria in an infected region of the body

That potential cannot be realized unless the nanoparticles can send some kind of signal back to the physician, in effect telling him or her exactly where the microscopic infection is located. The fact that these particles can actually send such a signal is the other reason why they work well in such cases. Put simply, they act as miniature sensors. For this reason, medical researchers have come to call them nanosensors. The reason the particles have this ability is because they can conduct electrical signals, a feature of many nanoparticles, including carbon nanotubes.

nanosensors

nanoparticles that can conduct and emit electrical signals

As part of their research into the use of nanosensors, Webster's team has grown clusters of carbon nanotubes on the surface of titanium hip implants. The nanotubes "can actually electrically sense what type of cell is attaching to the surface,"[24] says Webster. If the cells are bacteria in a newly forming infection, the nanotube sensors react in a certain way, almost as if they can sense it. A doctor's computerized electrical monitoring device then detects that reaction, confirming the infection's existence. According to medical reporter James McIntosh,

> Inbuilt into the sensor is a radio frequency that sends signals to an external computer, from which a clinician can access all of the information transmitted by the sensor. From this information, for example, a clinician can see whether the implant is free from bacteria, has a small amount of bacteria that the body will deal with, or a large number of bacteria requiring antibiotic treatment before a fully-fledged infection can take hold.[25]

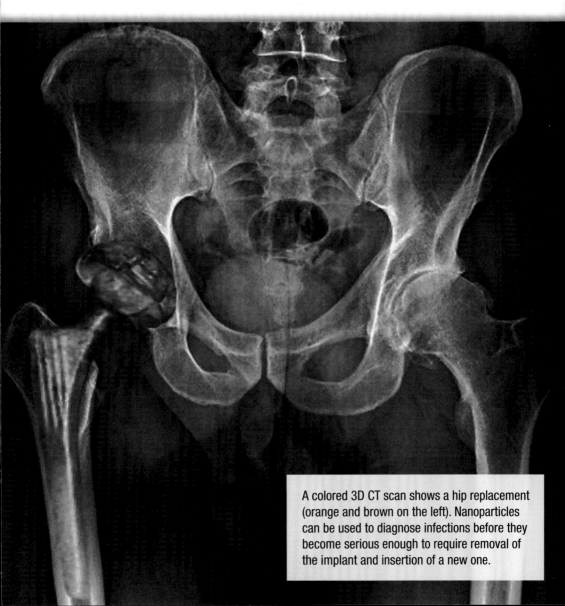

A colored 3D CT scan shows a hip replacement (orange and brown on the left). Nanoparticles can be used to diagnose infections before they become serious enough to require removal of the implant and insertion of a new one.

Clinical trials for Webster's nanosensors began in 2017 and were expected to continue into 2018. Numerous hospitals were expected to begin using them not long afterward.

Detecting Influenza and Other Viral Infections

Bacteria are not the only germs that cause infections and disease. Viruses, which are much smaller than bacteria, can penetrate almost all parts of the body and do much harm. Often a virus's presence is not diagnosed in time either to save a patient or at least to guarantee a speedy recovery. Several new diagnostic methods that employ nanoparticles are designed to diagnose viral illnesses. One of the most notorious and deadly viruses is the one that causes influenza, often called simply the flu. It wiped out millions of people during the early twentieth century and still claims between thirty thousand and fifty thousand victims each year worldwide.

Work on a new way to diagnose the flu virus has been pioneered by researchers at the University of Georgia. There, scientists Ralph Tripp and Jeremy Driskell have managed to merge the positive effects of antibodies and nanoparticles. (Antibodies are proteins that the immune system uses to attack disease cells.) "We've known for a long time that you can use antibodies to capture viruses and that nanoparticles have different traits based on their size," says Tripp. "What we've done is combine the two to create a diagnostic test that is rapid and highly sensitive."[26]

According to Driskell, the nanoparticles he and Tripp have used are made of gold, which is highly efficient at scattering light. In contrast, living molecules, including viruses, do not reflect light very well. When the combined antibodies and nanoparticles encounter the flu virus, therefore, the scattered light produces ebbs and flows in a predictable and measurable pattern. All that is needed to obtain this information is a simple test that can be done in a doctor's office or hospital. Driskell explains, "You take your sample, put it in the [monitoring] instrument, hit a button and get your results."[27]

Another diagnostic test intended to detect viral infections was developed by Charles M. Lieber at Harvard University. The process uses very thin silicon wires, dubbed nanowires. Like carbon nanotubes, the nanowires can emit electrical signals. Lieber's

The Types of Nanoparticles Used in Diagnosis

Research into the use of nanotechnology for medical diagnosis has involved many different nanoparticles. Two of the more common types are gold and silver nanoparticles and carbon and silicon nanotubes. Gold and silver nanoparticles have a number of uses in identifying diseases and other illnesses. They have proven particularly effective in imaging techniques, especially in magnetic resonance imaging. Used in small quantities, these particles appear to be largely nontoxic to the body. Meanwhile, carbon and silicon nanotubes have also shown to have low toxicity and are therefore considered relatively safe to ingest in small quantities. These long, hollow, cylindrical structures consist of one, two, or more layers of atoms, with rounded caps at the ends of the cylinders. They possess excellent electronic properties, including the ability to conduct electrical signals. Nanotubes are useful in diagnosing infectious diseases in part because they can detect and bind with proteins and other biomolecules. After they have attached themselves to proteins, nanotubes alter their electrical signals, which a doctor's monitor detects and measures, thereby identifying the illness involved.

wires turn on or off, electrically speaking, when exposed to a specific virus. The wires can also recognize the differences among several kinds of viruses. Tripp's, Lieber's, and other similar tests that employ nanoparticles are expected to begin wide use in hospitals by 2020 or soon thereafter.

Graphene's Atoms Detect Hepatitis

Another illness that kills many people each year is hepatitis. A disease affecting the liver, it takes several forms, usually designated hepatitis A, B, or C. Almost 400 million people contract one of these forms of hepatitis every year, and more than 1.4 million of them die. Until recently, diagnosing hepatitis required a blood test. That approach has a serious drawback—namely that it takes five to seven days to get the results. During that period the infected individuals are still contagious and often continue to spread the illness.

Scientists have long searched for a quicker diagnostic test for hepatitis. Because approximately 40 percent of the hepatitis-related deaths each year occur in China, it is perhaps not surprising that a Chinese lab developed a promising new test expected to be in wide use within a few years. The University of Chongqing in southwestern China sponsored the research, working in conjunction with scientists at Swansea University in the United Kingdom.

This new approach utilizes graphene, a type of carbon that is a cousin of buckyballs and nanotubes. Graphene consists of a thin layer of carbon atoms that form a lattice, or web. The layer is only a single atom in thickness, which places any given section of it in the ultra-microscopic nano realm.

Like fullerenes and nanotubes, graphene conducts electrical signals, which the new test takes advantage of. The researchers found a way to make the graphene lattice recognize human antibodies that attack hepatitis. When signals from the graphene indicate that those antibodies are present, it can only mean that hepatitis germs are also there, constituting a kind of indirect detection. Moreover, the graphene can be modified to recognize all three forms of hepatitis.

graphene

a type of carbon consisting of interconnected atoms that form a lattice only a single atom thick

Detecting an Impending Asthma Attack

Graphene-based nanosensors also lie at the heart of a new diagnostic test for another common illness—asthma. Causing swelling within the trachea, or airway, which seriously hinders breathing, asthma affects some 300 million people worldwide. Typical symptoms are shortness of breath, coughing, wheezing, and chest tightness. Roughly 17.7 million adults and 6.3 million children in the United States were diagnosed with asthma in 2014.

Present diagnostic tools for detecting an imminent asthma attack are unable tell how serious the episode will be. Moreover, the equipment involved is bulky and difficult for a patient to carry around. In 2016 researchers at Rutgers University in New Jersey decided to try to rectify these problems. The team, headed by scientist Mehdi Javanmard, set out "to develop a device that someone with asthma or another respiratory disease can wear around their neck or on their wrist." The person would "blow into it periodically to predict the onset of an asthma attack."[28]

Graphene (pictured in a computer illustration) is an atomic scale honeycomb lattice made of carbon atoms. Because graphene conducts electrical signals, it can be used to recognize and signal the presence of hepatitis antibodies.

In 2017 Javanmard and his colleagues announced their creation of nanosensors that can diagnose the onset of an asthma attack. They mixed oxygen with graphene, producing graphene oxide. Nanosensors made of the latter substance were then coaxed to detect minute levels of a chemical normally found in the breath of a person about to have an asthma attack. Javanmard says he expects a portable device using this technology to be commercially available by 2022.

The Future of Nanotech in Diagnosis

The ability to better detect an impending asthma attack and to identify hepatitis, the flu, and various infections represents only a few of the many examples of the growing potential of nanotechnology in medical diagnosis. Webster's nanosensors, Lieber's

Using Nanoparticles to Predict Peanut Allergy

In 2017 researchers at the University of Notre Dame in Indiana announced that they had used nanotechnology to develop an effective new method of diagnosing a potential peanut allergy. Studies have shown that more than 3 million Americans are allergic to nuts and that about 150 Americans die from nut and other food allergies each year. A peanut allergy is one of the more dangerous of these, and the people it affects rarely outgrow it. Medical researchers have long sought a diagnostic test that would detect the potential for infants to later develop a peanut allergy. Existing food allergy diagnostic tests are either risky (because they sometimes cause an adverse physical reaction) or do not provide enough information about how severe an allergy might become.

The Notre Dame scientists designed nanoparticles that mimic the peanut allergen. (Allergens are tiny natural substances that cause allergies.) The nanoparticles display each element of the allergen on their surfaces one at a time. Dubbed nanoallergens, these fake allergens induce a minor allergic response in those patients who are prone to the allergy. But that response is tiny and harmless. Nevertheless, the test indicates whether the person is at risk of developing the allergy. "We are currently working with allergy specialist clinicians," says one of the Notre Dame scientists, Basar Bilgicer. After further testing, "ultimately our vision is to take this technology and make it available to all people who suffer from food allergies."

Quoted in Jessica Sieff, "Novel Platform Uses Nanoparticles to Detect Peanut Allergies," Phys.org, June 26, 2017. https://phys.org.

nanowires, and Tripp's improved flu test will be used in hospitals worldwide in the next few years. But what about twenty, forty, and fifty years from now? How will the use of nanoparticles of various kinds have transformed the process of diagnosis by then?

First, the use of nanoparticles made of silicon, carbon, and other materials to detect viral infections will become far more sophisticated. Already Lieber and other researchers have managed to identify two, three, or four separate viruses in a single test. These scientists predict that within twenty years a few nanowires or other types of nanosensors will be able to see and identify thousands of different viruses that could at one time or another infect a patient. This will allow doctors to diagnose viral infections and diseases in their very earliest stages, when curing them is still relatively easy.

Yet fifty or sixty years from now, even that impressive diagnostic ability may well seem rudimentary. Linda Williams and Wade Adams write, "Picture a small plastic chip the size of your thumbnail. Imagine that most of the diagnostic lab tests that take days to weeks to get results today could be done in a few minutes in your doctor's office using this chip. Is this mere far-out science fiction? Not at all. A new nanotechnology concept makes it possible."[29]

That concept builds on technologies already either in use or under development today in labs, including silicon microchips and nanowires. Each future nanowire inserted into the body will be coated with a probe composed of specific proteins or antibodies. Information about the body's inner nano realm provided by those molecules will be conveyed via electrical signals to the chip, which the doctor will look at to make the diagnosis. "The lab chips of the future," Williams and Adams continue, could test for "thousands of chemical compounds, byproducts, and particles. They would allow for the creation of a universal test for nearly everything from a single patient sample. The days of being 'stuck' several times for a variety of tests would be gone."[30]

CHAPTER 3

Nanoscale Delivery of Medicines

Today one of the more prevalent, as well as promising, medical applications for nanotechnology uses nanoparticles to carry medicines into the body. Most doctors, scientists, and researchers refer to this approach as nanotechnology and drug delivery. Although a number of drug delivery methods of this kind are in the research stage, others have already seen practical application in hospitals and other medical settings.

In fact, this was one of the first areas in medicine to use nanotechnology. Doctors used liposomes and micelles to carry microscopic amounts of medicines as early as the 1960s. That practice carried on into the 1970s and 1980s. Liposomes are tiny round sacs that usually enclose a few to several water molecules. Micelles are microscopic structures that transform into spherical groups of molecules when in contact with liquids. Technicians injected molecules of certain drugs into these miniature sacs and spheres. In turn, they inserted the liposomes and micelles into specific body parts to achieve a therapeutic, or healing, effect.

For many years no one, including the doctors in question, saw these techniques as part of the science of nanotechnology. This was largely because terms like *nanotechnology*, *nanotubes*, and *nanosensors* did not come into widespread use until the 1990s and the decade that followed. Nevertheless, these were some of the beginnings of nanotechnology's use in medicine.

Since then, researchers and doctors have developed ultra-microscopic particles and structures to deliver drugs to the body in increasingly sophisticated ways. This method can provide diabetics with the insulin they require to remain healthy and can also help to treat diseases of the eye. In addition, nanotechnology can aid doctors in treating people suffering from arthritis. Moreover, the National Aeronautics and Space Administration (NASA) has developed nanocapsules, which are tiny vessels that deliver medicine to astronauts to protect them from prolonged exposure to radiation.

liposomes

microscopic round-shaped sacs that usually enclose a few to several water molecules

The Drawbacks of Traditional Methods

Doctors and other medical experts began to turn to microscopic medicine delivery systems because traditional systems have a number of drawbacks. First, the two most widely used of those older systems—oral (swallowing a pill or liquid) and intravascular (getting a shot in the arm from a syringe, or needle)—are not site-specific delivery methods. That is, they do not target the place in the body that needs therapy.

micelles

microscopic structures that transform into spherical groups of molecules when in contact with liquids

If a person has a bacterial infection in his or her leg, for instance, a doctor might prescribe an antibiotic to kill the germs and thereby eliminate the infection. If the patient takes the antibiotic in pill form, that pill goes down his or her esophagus to the stomach and intestines, where it breaks down into molecular form. Those molecules soon reach the bloodstream, which distributes them throughout the body. A few of the antibacterial molecules do reach the target site in the leg and begin fighting the infection, but most of them end up in other parts of the body, where their potential healing properties are wasted.

Another drawback of traditional drug delivery methods is that the medicines delivered throughout the body do not readily discern the difference between good and bad bacteria. While the drugs are attacking the harmful bacteria that are causing an infection, they also are attacking beneficial germs in other parts of the body.

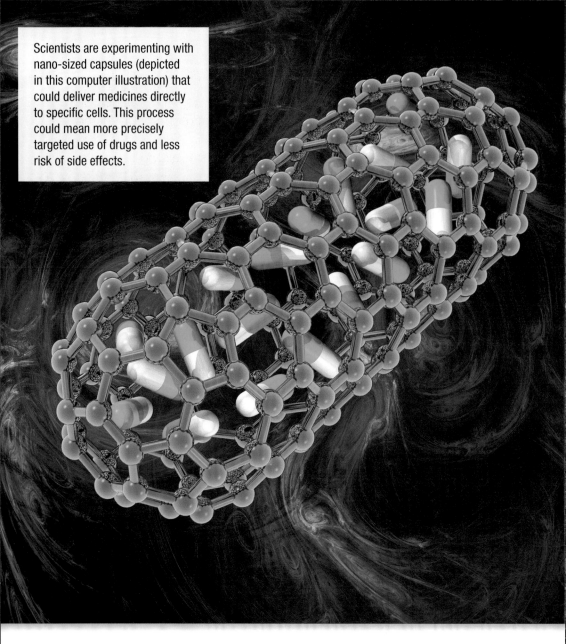

Scientists are experimenting with nano-sized capsules (depicted in this computer illustration) that could deliver medicines directly to specific cells. This process could mean more precisely targeted use of drugs and less risk of side effects.

The Advantages of Nanoscale Drug Carriers

In marked contrast, drug delivery using nanoscale capsules or particles eliminates most of those drawbacks. Employing nanotechnology to carry medicines into the body allows for more precise targeting, less waste, less risk of side effects, and a higher drug-loading capacity. These advantages are due in part to the tiny size of the medicine carriers. The typical target of the therapeutic drugs that a doctor prescribes is a specific mass of human cells. On average, cells measure about ten thousand nanometers across.

To most effectively target cells of that size, the drug carriers should be considerably smaller, and that is always the case when using nanoparticles. In fact, those minuscule structures are in the same size range as proteins, which are among the tiniest facets of the microscopic realm within the body. The average protein, including hemoglobin, the protein in red blood cells that carries oxygen throughout the body, is roughly five nanometers across, two thousand times smaller than a cell. Compare that to the more commonly employed nanoscale drug carriers. A liposome can range from twenty to two hundred nanometers across; and a micelle is even smaller, at two to twenty nanometers in diameter. Thus, the nanoscale drug carriers measure from about fifty to four thousand times smaller than an average cell.

Thanks to its tiny size, each nanoparticle can find a comfortable place to make contact with a cell's membrane, or outer surface. From there, the carrier crosses through the membrane and enters the cell, where its organelles and other inner components immediately begin absorbing the medicine. According to one biomedical researcher,

> The small size of nanoparticles allows them to interact readily with biomolecules on the cell surface and within the cell, and thus allows better understanding of complex processes that govern the behavior of cells in their normal state and during the diseased state. Nanoscale drug delivery systems have the ability to cross cell membranes. Thus, the drug can be delivered to specific organelles inside the cell.[31]

Furthermore, liposomes and other nanoscale drug carriers have another advantage over traditional medicine delivery methods. When a doctor-prescribed medicine in pill or liquid form enters the stomach, powerful enzymes and other so-called stomach acids immediately go to work. They degrade a certain portion of the medicine before it can even reach the bloodstream. In contrast, liposomes, dendrimers (nanoparticles with an inner core surrounded by branch-like structures), and other nanoscale drug carriers possess outer shells. Those coverings are tough enough to protect the medicine inside them from destruction by stomach acids.

Targeting Bacteria and Heart Disease

The applications of nanoscale drug carriers are many and varied. Moreover, existing uses continue to be refined through new research and experimentation. Using nanoparticles to deliver antibacterial medicines to infected body parts is a clear example. Doctors have employed liposomes carrying antibiotics for years. But the materials and techniques involved continue to advance.

In 2015, for example, scientists at the Massachusetts Institute of Technology (MIT) announced a breakthrough. They knew that even some of the existing nanoscale drug carriers met with difficulty if the germs they encountered had developed resistance to antibiotics. The MIT researchers constructed nanoparticles having two layers of molecules surrounding a hollow inner core. The outer layer was composed of a chemical that protected the payload of powerful antibiotics in the core. The inner layer was made up of a strongly acidic substance. After reaching the tar-

Nanodiamonds and Glaucoma

Using nanotechnology to battle the eye disease glaucoma has been the target of much research in the past two decades. That ailment frequently creates pressure in the eye due to a buildup of fluid. The standard way of treating glaucoma is to administer drops of fluid that induce the eye to get rid of some of the fluid. However, the drops sometimes produce unwanted side effects, including blurred vision, stinging, itching, and headaches; for this reason, patients often have trouble remaining on the dosing schedules their doctors have given them.

In 2014 scientists at the University of Southern California's school of dentistry announced their invention of a drug delivery system that appears to cause less severe side effects than traditional glaucoma medicines. It also helps patients stay on their schedules. The researchers combined glaucoma-fighting drugs with microscopic diamonds—dubbed nanodiamonds—and inserted them into the fabric of contact lenses. Each nanodiamond is about five nanometers in diameter and is shaped like a miniature soccer ball. The medicine stored within the tiny diamonds releases into the eye when the diamonds come in contact with the patient's tears. Because this system delivers the needed drugs into the eye a little at a time, the patient no longer has to worry about when to take his or her eye drops. As an added bonus, the compound containing the nanodiamonds makes the contact lenses more durable, so they last longer than standard ones.

In this computer illustration, a stent holds open an artery to help ensure blood flow. Researchers are developing nanoparticles that can deliver drugs to damaged or clogged arteries without the need for invasive procedures.

geted area, the acidic molecules enhanced the antibiotics, and their combined effect destroyed the drug-resistant bacteria.

A different sort of direct drug delivery shows promise for fighting heart disease, which is the leading cause of death in the United States. According to the Centers for Disease Control and Prevention, about 610,000 Americans die of heart disease each year, accounting for one of every four deaths overall in the country. A chief cause of heart disease is damaged and/or clogged arteries, especially those located near the heart. At present, one common method of treating such distressed arteries is to implant tube-shaped supports called stents. A stent holds an artery open, helping ensure good blood flow, and releases a therapeutic drug into the bloodstream. Although this approach often works, insertion of one of more stents is considered an invasive procedure.

In 2014 scientists at Clemson University in South Carolina developed nanoparticles that can deliver drugs to damaged arteries using a noninvasive approach. This method takes advantage of the fact that when the elastic fibers in an artery get damaged, small hook-like structures appear on their surfaces. These hooks readily accept molecules of any medicine that can be targeted to that location. The Clemson researchers coated their nanoscale drug carriers with a sticky protein designed to latch onto the tiny hooks in the damaged arterial wall. In the words of one of the scientists involved, Naren Vyavahare, "We developed nanoparticles that have antibodies on the surface that attach to diseased sites like Velcro. Interestingly, these newly created nanoparticles only accumulate at the damaged artery, not in the healthy arteries, enabling site-specific drug delivery."[32]

Another benefit of the nanoparticles in question is that they produce a more long-lasting healing effect. According to one of the Clemson researchers, "These nanoparticles can be delivered intravenously [through a vein] to target injured areas and can administer drugs over longer periods of time, thus avoiding repeated surgical interventions at the disease site."[33]

Nanotechnology to Aid Diabetes Patients

Another intravenous delivery of nanoparticles containing life-sustaining medicine has been developed by researchers at North Carolina State University, working with colleagues at the University of North Carolina at Chapel Hill, MIT, and Children's Hospital Boston. In this case, the treatment is for type 1 diabetes, which affects an estimated 1.2 million Americans.

In this form of diabetes, the body does not produce insulin, normally manufactured in the pancreas. Researchers Earl and Nancy Boysen explain what insulin is and the drawbacks of present methods of treating diabetes:

> When a patient has type 1 diabetes, his or her body does not produce sufficient insulin, a hormone that transports glucose, or blood sugar, from the bloodstream into the body's cells. This can cause a host of [negative] health effects. Currently, diabetes patients must take frequent blood samples to monitor their blood-sugar levels and inject insulin as needed to ensure their blood sugar levels are in the "normal" range. However, these injections can be painful, and it can be difficult to determine the accurate dose level of insulin. Administering too much or too little insulin poses its own health risks.[34]

Maintaining Health in Space

NASA announced an important breakthrough in 2012—the use of nanotechnology to improve the health of astronauts traveling in space. Scientists at the agency explained that one of the main dangers in space is exposure to high levels of radiation. When astronauts go into orbit or to the moon, and someday to Mars, they are showered by intense radiation from both the sun and cosmic rays (high-energy particles mostly originating outside the solar system). Such radiation can damage bone marrow and destroy the human immune system.

To combat this problem, NASA researchers led by David Loftus created a so-called biocapsule. This drug delivery system is constructed of carbon nanotubes that, thanks to their unique layered structure, are resistant to most kinds of radiation. Some of the capsules can be tailored to release drugs meant to treat various other ailments as well. According to science and technology writer Brent Rose, these tiny nanoparticles "will be able to diagnose and instantly treat an astronaut without him or her even knowing there's something amiss." Rose characterizes this technology as an important medical advance. "Picture this: An astronaut is going to Mars. The round-trip journey will take between two and three years. During that time, the astronaut will not have access to a doctor, [so] prior to launch, the astronaut is implanted with a number of NASA biocapsules. The astronaut's body is equipped to deal with a whole host of problems on its own."

Brent Rose, "The Miraculous NASA Breakthrough That Could Save Millions of Lives," Gizmodo, February 8, 2012. http://gizmodo.com.

In 2013 the North Carolina State University team announced its success in creating what it calls a smart system in which nanoparticles carrying insulin are introduced into the body as needed. The system begins in the same way that current treatments do—with the patient monitoring his or her blood sugar levels. If those levels are too low, the patient makes a painless injection of a solution into the skin of a leg, arm, or elsewhere. That solution contains a mass of nanoparticles enclosed in a capsule made of a safe, biodegradable chemical substance. The capsule carries its insulin payload in its center, protected by a tough outer coating.

The nanoparticles carrying the insulin do not travel right into the bloodstream, as happens in standard insulin injections. Instead, they remain in the skin and slowly diffuse a little at a time through the capillaries (tiny blood vessels in the skin) into the bloodstream. This allows for a slow, steady stream of insulin that lasts up to ten days or more. "This technology effectively creates a 'closed-loop' system that mimics the activity of the pancreas in a healthy person," says one of the leaders of the research team, Zhen Gu. The system releases "insulin in response to glucose level changes. This has the potential to improve the health and quality of life of diabetes patients."[35] The team has already moved into clinical trials on humans and expects the new technology to be in use in hospitals sometime between 2018 and 2020.

Vaccines and the Future

Just as the encapsulated nanoparticles provide a better way to deliver insulin, a new delivery system involving nanotechnology offers an alternate way to deliver vaccines into the body. Vaccines are substances that help the body develop immunity to various diseases. Usually doctors administer vaccines via needle injections, which can be painful.

nanopatch

a new device consisting of a patch the size of a postage stamp that uses thousands of tiny projections to painlessly deliver a vaccine to a patient

In 2016 Mark Kendall of the University of Queensland in Australia publicized the results of his research into a painless and more efficient delivery system for vaccines. It consists of a skin patch called the nanopatch. It contains tens of thousands of microscopic projections, each containing thousands of molecules of a desired vaccine. According to one expert observer,

Rather than a needle, the vaccine is given through a patch that looks like a small Band-Aid. This may not make needles obsolete, but can instead provide an alternative for those that don't want an injection. The patch targets immune-rich cells on the outer layer of the skin with different micro projections. No longer would you need an injection that goes inches deep. These micro projections release just beneath the skin. The vaccines themselves are dry and coated on the patch. The coating releases almost immediately upon making contact with the skin.[36]

Many medical experts believe that vaccines will be delivered via devices like the nanopatch in the near future. As for the somewhat more distant future of the mid-twenty-first century, a number of scientists foresee that nanorobots, also called nanobots, will revolutionize medicine, including the field of drug delivery. These microscopic devices will be semi-intelligent in the sense

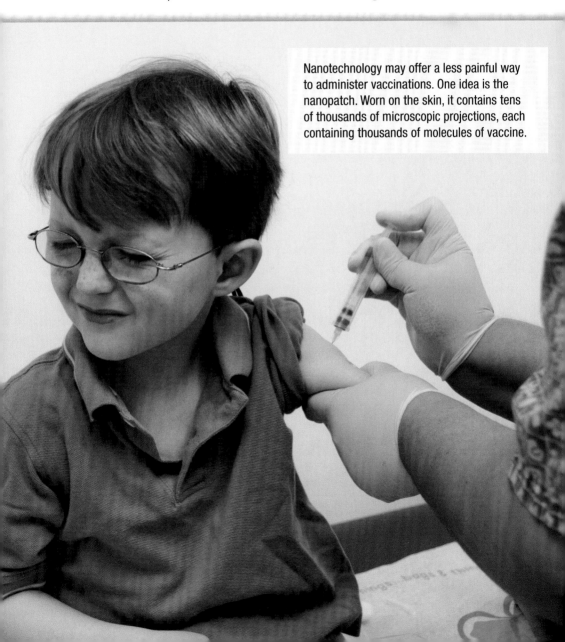

Nanotechnology may offer a less painful way to administer vaccinations. One idea is the nanopatch. Worn on the skin, it contains tens of thousands of microscopic projections, each containing thousands of molecules of vaccine.

that they will be programmable and able to remember how to perform numerous tasks. Moreover, they will not merely carry medicines to targeted sites. They also will be able to manufacture some of those drugs within the body, using various existing molecules in the cells and blood. Scientist K.H. Hassan Reza and his colleagues at India's C.L. Baid Metha College of Pharmacy explain that such nanorobots "will have enhanced mobile characteristics, and will be able to transport themselves as well as other objects to desired locations at nano-scale."[37] Moreover, some nanorobots will be able to gather various loose molecules floating between the organs and use them to assemble new nanostructures within the body. These tiny constructions will become miniature storehouses for medicines brought to them by drug-carrying nanoparticles. The storehouses will release the medicines a little at a time, as needed.

According to Reza, a number of scientists are already working on developing these tiny robotic machines. "Several substantial steps have been taken by great researchers all over the world," he says, "and are contributing to this ever challenging and exciting field."[38]

CHAPTER 4

Curing Cancer

The use of nanoparticles to deliver insulin to diabetics is already being tested on human subjects. So is using these microscopic wonders to deliver vaccines to provide people immunity to dozens of diseases. A majority of medical researchers agree that by 2020 or shortly thereafter, the treatment of these and numerous other illnesses will be revolutionized by the fast-emerging science of nanotechnology.

Yet as important as it will be to overcome so many ailments that have long plagued humanity, that major achievement will, remarkably, be eclipsed by another that looms on the horizon. Considered the holy grail of nanomedicine, and of medicine in general, it is the conquest of the dreaded scourge of cancer. In recent years nanotechnology has shown astonishing promise for both diagnosing cancer and helping to cure that disease through the delivery of highly targeted cancer-fighting medicines.

A Modern Fantastic Voyage

Doctors and medical researchers seek every possible weapon against cancer, including nanotechnology, because the disease takes an enormous and frightening toll on humanity each year. The American Cancer Society estimated that in 2017, close to 1.7 million Americans would contract cancer and more than 600,000 of them would die of that illness. It remains the second most common cause of death in the country after heart disease.

Cancer occurs when normal cells are replaced by abnormal cells that grow at an accelerated rate. According to the National Cancer Institute in Bethesda, Maryland,

Cancer can start almost anywhere in the human body, which is made up of trillions of cells. Normally, human cells grow and divide to form new cells as the body needs them. When cells grow old or become damaged, they die, and new cells take their place. When cancer develops, however, this orderly process breaks down. As cells become more and more abnormal, old or damaged cells survive when they should die, and new cells form when they are not needed. These extra cells can divide without stopping and may form growths called tumors.[39]

The idea of using nanoparticles to treat and eradicate cancer conjures up memories of the famous 1966 film *Fantastic Voyage*. In what was then truly a fantastical story, an incredibly advanced machine shrinks a submarine-like vessel, the *Proteus*, along with its crew of scientists and doctors, to the size of a bacterium. The intrepid group then takes an incredible journey through a man's body. The goal is to reach and destroy a blood clot in his brain. During the trip, the miniaturized crew encounters various dangers, including attacks by white blood cells and antibodies dispatched by the patient's immune system.

Although the events depicted in *Fantastic Voyage* "were far-fetched when it was released," they are "now being realized every day in labs around the world," says *Stanford Medical Magazine*'s Krista Conger. This is particularly true "in cancer treatment," she points out.

> Nanotechnology is allowing researchers to manipulate molecules and structures much smaller than a single cell to enhance our ability to see, monitor, and destroy cancer cells in the body. Tens of thousands of patients have already received chemotherapy drugs delivered by nanoparticles called liposomes, [and] a few have been approved by the FDA [US Food and Drug Administration].[40]

One of those approved cancer drugs is Doxil. It contains millions of nanotubes that carry the drug doxorubicin inside their hollow centers. Doxil is mainly used in the treatment of ovarian cancer (cancer of the ovaries) and multiple myeloma (cancer of

In a scene from the 1966 movie *Fantastic Voyage*, miniaturized doctors travel through a man's body in hopes of destroying a blood clot in his brain. Although this idea is far-fetched, the use of nanoparticles to deliver chemotherapy drugs to cancer patients is not.

the plasma cells in the bone marrow, a key part of the body's immune system). Meanwhile, dozens of other cancer treatments based on nanoparticles are presently in clinical trials with either animals or humans. Experts estimate that the use of various kinds of nanomaterials to treat many kinds of cancer will soon be a reality. One of those experts, Sanjiv Sam Gambhir of the Stanford University School of Medicine, says that "nanotechnology offers an exquisite sensitivity and precision that is difficult to match with any other technology." He adds that "within the next decade [by 2026] nanomedicine will change the path of cancer diagnosis and treatment in this country."[41]

A New Way to Diagnose Cancer

One way that cancer specialists like Gambhir are using nanoparticles is to recognize the existence of cancer cells in the body earlier than was possible before nanotechnology appeared. "Early diagnosis is absolutely critical," Gambhir says, and current methods of diagnosis often miss the earliest signs of cancer. This is because cancer begins with only a handful of diseased cells, a group too small to detect using present imaging and other techniques. Yet when cancerous masses are discovered, they often contain millions of diseased cells. Precisely diagnosing cancer before it can form dangerous tumors "requires an entirely different type of approach and technology than we've relied on in the past. Without nanomedicine, we wouldn't have a chance of accomplishing [that] goal."[42]

Gambhir and other scientists have developed a number of different approaches to using nanoparticles to diagnose cancer. One of the most promising involves tailoring the particles in very specific ways. Here, as in other medical applications of these microscopic tools, scientists take advantage of the fact that certain nanoparticles conduct electrical charges. As a result, they can send out small but readable signals when they encounter specified targets.

In this case, the targets are cancer cells. Gambhir and his colleagues at Stanford managed to modify gold nanotubes as well as ball-shaped versions called nanospheres. Those particles were, in a sense, trained to latch onto, and stick to, any cancerous cells they encountered during their travels through the body. Having made contact that way, the nanotubes emitted a signal that Gambhir's instruments could readily detect. "We've specially designed nanoparticles that can send back a massively amplified, whopping signal when they bind to cancer cells,"[43] he says.

nanospheres

nanoparticles that are shaped like tiny balls

The large surface area of the gold nanotubes is advantageous when hunting down cancer cells. The bigger a microscopic particle's outer surface, the greater its likelihood of making contact with cancer cells. As an analogy, imagine a small pond containing one hundred fish that are swimming around randomly. If a fisherman dips a small net into the pond, he is likely to catch fewer fish than if he dips a large net into the pond.

Similarly, the gold nanoparticles have a great deal of outer surface area, far larger, in fact, than ordinary microscopic particles

Cancer Imaging Through Light and Sound

Sanjiv Sam Gambhir of the Stanford University School of Medicine here describes so-called photoacoustic medical imaging to diagnose cancer. In photoacoustic imaging, light produces sound via nanoparticles, including carbon-based nanotubes.

In photoacoustic imaging, light goes into the body [and] penetrate[s] deeply. That light interacts with a nanoparticle, and the nanoparticle then slightly heats, not enough to cause any damage, but slightly heats. And that heating produces a pressure wave [in the air] and therefore sound. So light in, sound out. And a nanoparticle can be designed so that it is very good at absorbing the light and very good therefore at producing sound. And the nanoparticle can be functionalized to go find tumors. Gold, as it turns out, is also a very good material for absorbing light and producing a strong photoacoustic signal. Also carbon-based molecules like nanotubes are very black and dark; they do a good job of absorbing light and therefore heat to produce sound. And several other nanoparticle strategies are on the horizon for this new emerging area of photoacoustic imaging. And these likely will translate in the clinic with applications of prostate cancer imaging, breast cancer imaging, things where you aren't trying to go too deep, but deep enough where light can go in and sound come back out, letting you get much better spatial resolution, much better sensitivity to detect smaller tumors than what is possible with other current imaging technologies.

Sanjiv Sam Gambhir, "Nanotechnology in Cancer Imaging," NCI Alliance for Nanotechnology in Cancer, December 17, 2010, podcast. https://nano.cancer.gov.

that are much bigger. This may at first seem contrary to logic. One would assume that a larger particle would have more surface area. Yet the truth is exactly the opposite. An object's surface area is measured in square units, and one calculates it by adding together the areas of its faces. But if one breaks that object up into a thousand pieces, much more surface area than before becomes exposed. Therefore, one large object has considerably less surface area than many smaller objects. This effect is marked enough in objects visible to the eye and low-power microscopes. But when one reaches the nano realm, the effect becomes hugely magnified. In Conger's words, most nanoparticles have "tremendous amounts of surface area as compared with larger particles.

Gold nanospheres (depicted in an illustration) are designed to latch onto cancer cells as they journey through the body. Once they make contact, they emit signals that confirm the presence of cancer at the very earliest stages.

A cube of gold with sides 1 centimeter [0.4 in] long has a total surface area of 6 square centimeters [smaller than a postage stamp]. But the same volume filled with gold nanospheres with diameters of 1 nanometer has a surface area greater than half a football field."[44]

Gambhir and his colleagues found that gold nanoparticles, thanks to their extraordinary amount of surface area, detect cancer cells more efficiently than traditional methods. In fact, those scientists say, this technique has the potential to diagnose cancer even when only a few diseased cells are present. Traditional cancer diagnostic methods simply cannot detect the supermicroscopic beginnings of a cancerous tumor. Gambhir explains, "It's not that our therapies are poor—it's that we apply them too late. Nanotechnology has the potential to [identify] early cancer cells present in the hundreds or thousands versus the billions already present in currently diagnosable tumors."[45]

Targeted Treatment

Another major advantage of using nanoparticles to deal with cancer, Gambhir points out, "is that they themselves can . . . be both diagnostic and therapeutic. So if you are going to bother to image a tumor and send a particle in that can go hunt down an abnormal [tumor] cell, why not also have the particle be a therapeutic [tool] as well?"[46]

Some scientists began working on a practical application of that idea—using tiny particles to target cancer cells—during the 1970s. These efforts eventually paid off. By the early 1990s the FDA had begun to approve the use of liposomes and similar nanoscale structures to deliver drugs to cancer patients. Since that time more than a dozen substances have been approved to battle cancer in this manner. "From a practical perspective, nano-based techniques aren't the wave of the future," remarks Stanford researcher Heather Wakelee. "This is the now. And it's changing how we treat patients in the clinic."[47]

Of the several advantages of employing nanotechnology in the fight against cancer, perhaps the key one is that the approach is highly targeted. Overall it affects only the cancer cells. In comparison, traditional methods, such as radiation and chemotherapy—using chemical substances to battle cancer—can adversely affect the entire body.

A well-known negative result of radiation and chemotherapy is a patient's temporary loss of hair. In the words of Andrew Tsourkas, a bioengineering expert at the University of Pennsylvania, "One of the main issues for current chemotherapies is that they distribute nonspecifically throughout the body." As a result, "you end up with these adverse effects because you're hitting targets that you'd rather avoid." In traditional chemotherapy, a doctor cannot choose exactly where the medicine goes, so healthy cells receive a dose of it as well. Thus, Tsourkas concludes, "You get a lot of off-target toxicity."[48]

Combining Nanoparticles and DNA

Numerous scientists in labs around the world have been searching for years for ways to avoid such undesirable effects. Among the more successful of these efforts is the one conducted by a team of University of Toronto scientists headed by Professor Warren Chan.

Could Some Nanoparticles Be Toxic?

Although various applications of nanotechnology hold huge promise for treating cancer and other diseases, injecting nanoparticles into the human body might have some risks. As scientists Buddolla Viswanath and Sanghyo Kim explain here, research continues into those particles' possible toxic side effects, which are still largely unclear.

Nanotoxicology and nano-risk have been drawing increasing attention of toxicologists and regulatory scientists as the manufacturing of nanomaterials increases. . . . A number of hazardous exposure conditions are encountered by the workers occupied in nanotechnology activities. In fact, nanomaterials may have significant, still unknown, hazards, properties that can pose risks for a broad range of workers: researchers, laboratory technicians, cleaners, production workers, transportation, storage and retail workers, [and others]. . . . It is essential to know the toxicity of nano material before using it for a variety of applications. . . . In addition, the effects and impacts on human health need to be reviewed accordingly.

The International Council on Nanotechnology (ICON) has created a database of all the publications of several nano materials along with their impact on environmental health and safety. . . . The utmost challenge faced in the field of nanotoxicology now-a-days is the recognition as well as the estimation of the [possible] deleterious [harmful] effects of a variety of engineered nanomaterials.

Buddolla Viswanath and Sanghyo Kim, "Influence of Nanotoxicity on Human Health and Environment: The Alternative Strategies," *Review of Environmental Contamination and Toxicology,* vol. 242, 2017, p. 63. http://9783319512426-c1%20(1).pdf.

The team's main goal has been to find ways to deliver chemotherapy medicines directly into tumors while leaving other body parts unaffected. "Your body is basically a series of compartments," Chan explains. "Think of it as a giant house with rooms inside. We're trying to figure out how to get something that's outside into one specific room. One has to develop a map and a system that can move through the house where each path to the final room may have different restrictions such as height and width."[49]

Chan and his team have succeeded in attaching nanoparticles to strands of DNA, the complex molecule that carries a person's genetic code, or physical blueprint. The resulting nanoparticles can change their shape, size, and even their chemistry to a degree. This makes them far more flexible than many other nanoparticles. These "shape-changing nanoparticles," Chan states, are very much like "a series of building blocks, kind of like a LEGO set."[50] In other words, the particles can be altered and reconstructed into numerous shapes to be used as needed in carrying drugs that will directly attack various cancer cells.

The University of Toronto team's work was published in 2016 in the prestigious journal *Proceedings of the National Academy of Sciences*. In response to international interest in the team's achievement, Chan explained that he was inspired by the natural ability of proteins, large molecules that perform numerous functions in the body, to alter their shape. "Using this idea," he recalled,

> we thought, "Can we engineer a nanoparticle to function like a protein, but one that can be programmed outside the body with medical capabilities?" [We have] only scratched the surface of how nanotechnology "delivery" works in the body, so now we're continuing to explore different details of why and how tumors and other organs allow or block certain things from getting in.[51]

Drugs Activated by Light and Diamonds

Another promising way to employ nanoparticles against cancer cells was pioneered at the Wellman Center for Photomedicine at Massachusetts General Hospital in Boston. The process is called photodynamic therapy (PDT). It involves using light to trigger a chemical reaction that in turn releases a powerful anticancer drug.

The researchers who developed PDT began with nanoparticles they had injected with a specific chemical, known as a photosensitizer. Then they exposed the particles to specific wavelengths of light. That exposure caused the photosensitizer to chemically react and release molecules that can disrupt a cancer cell's ability to grow and spread. One of the

photodynamic

relating to inducing a reaction to light, as in a therapy that uses light to help deliver powerful anticancer drugs to cancer patients

photosensitizer

a chemical that, when exposed to certain wavelengths of light, reacts by releasing molecules that can disrupt a cancer cell's ability to grow and spread

lead scientists at the Wellman Center, Bryan Spring, told an interviewer, "The new optically active nanoparticle we have developed is able [to] achieve tumor photo-damage." The new process, he added, opens up "new possibilities for synchronized multidrug combination therapies and tumor-focused drug release."[52]

Experts believe that photodynamic therapy will likely be effective in treating several different forms of cancer. Meanwhile, researchers at the Jonsson Comprehensive Cancer Center at the University of California, Los Angeles (UCLA), have developed a drug delivery method designed more specifically to target brain cancer. Scientist Dean Ho and his UCLA colleagues chose as their foe the most common and lethal type of brain tumor—glioblastoma. Using traditional anticancer treatments, including surgery, radiation, and chemotherapy, most glioblastoma patients survive less than a year and a half after diagnosis. This type of cancer is so hard to treat partly because anticancer drugs usually cannot get through the thick mass of blood vessels that surround and protect the brain.

glioblastoma

the most common and lethal type of brain cancer

Ho and his team skirted this problem by using supermicroscopic nanodiamonds. They coated the exteriors of these particles with molecules of the chemotherapy drug doxorubicin. Those molecules formed a surprisingly tight bond with the nanodiamonds' multifaceted surfaces. When injected into cancer cells, the diamonds stayed put there because the cells could not eject them. That ensured that the drug would dose the cells at full strength, a feat never attained in traditional treatments. In this situation, Ho says, "nanotechnology actually helps chemotherapy function better, making it easier on the patient and harder on the cancer."[53]

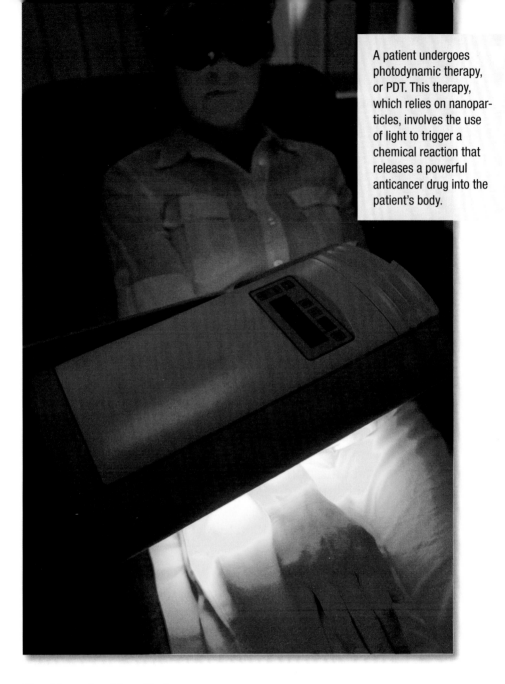

A patient undergoes photodynamic therapy, or PDT. This therapy, which relies on nanoparticles, involves the use of light to trigger a chemical reaction that releases a powerful anticancer drug into the patient's body.

Further in the Future

The nanotechnology cancer treatment methods developed by doctors Chan, Spring, Ho, and their respective teams are expected to come into common use in hospitals sometime between 2020 and 2025. The same can be said for many dozens of other similar lines of anticancer research going on in labs around the world. In fact, says Christine Peterson, cofounder of the Foresight Institute, which studies and promotes the possible uses of nanotechnology, the expansion of cancer research using nano-materials has exploded in recent years. "Big efforts have gone into exploiting nanotech for dealing with cancer," she states. That has included funding to the tune of many "hundreds of millions of dollars. And those efforts are working."[54]

According to Peterson, some of the projects in question are still experimental. Such efforts are not expected to bear significant fruit for many years. For example, she says, scientists are developing nanoparticles that emit "a detectable color signal when a cancer cell is found."[55] Other nanoparticles, Peterson adds, could someday be paired with tools such as magnets or sound vibrations to oppose and eradicate cancer.

Nanoparticles hold such great promise in part because they are structurally unique, strong, and tremendously flexible, say Gambhir and one of his colleagues, Avnesh S. Thakor. Those miniature pieces of matter, visible only in the most powerful microscopes, "are able to bind, absorb, and carry other compounds such as small molecule drugs, DNA, RNA, proteins, and [various microscopic] probes. Furthermore, their size, shape, and surface characteristics enable them to have high stability."[56]

These attributes bode well for the future of humanity's fight against one of its most despised enemies, Gambhir and Thakor point out. "With our continued drive to cure cancer," they say, "and our determination to understand the molecular mechanisms that drive this disease, nanotechnology provides hope in developing new ways to diagnose, treat, and follow patients with cancer in the 21st century."[57]

CHAPTER 5

Nanoparticles Rebuild Bodily Tissues

The concept of rebuilding and restoring damaged body parts has haunted people's imaginations ever since English novelist Mary Shelley published her classic book *Frankenstein* in 1818. In that morbid but fascinating story, brilliant scientist Victor Frankenstein successfully pieces together body parts from deceased individuals and gives them new life in a reanimated corpse. For a long time rebuilding damaged or dead bodily tissues remained, like Frankenstein's so-called monster, only science fiction.

Yet the relentless advance of science was destined eventually to transform fiction into reality. For example, the idea of transplanting a dead person's heart into a living individual was considered impossible until surgeons managed to do just that during the mid-twentieth century. Similarly, the widespread and seemingly miraculous uses of nanoparticles that Richard Feynman predicted in 1959 started to become reality during the early years of the twenty-first century. In the words of the Foresight Institute's Christine Peterson, "As science and technology advance, the world looks more and more like science fiction, and advanced nanotechnology is definitely a big driver in that direction."[58] Nowhere is that statement truer than in the ways that nanotechnology is presently revolutionizing the medical discipline of tissue engineering.

Traditional Ways to Rebuild Skin

Even before scientists began experimenting with nanoparticles in labs, significant strides had been made in tissue engineering. Indeed, by the late twentieth century medical researchers had begun to develop ways of rebuilding damaged tissues, especially those making up the skin. The body's largest organ, the skin protects the inner organs from physical damage and disease and aids in regulating body temperature. A person's skin is made up of two principal layers. The outer one—the epidermis—is composed mostly of ordinary skin cells, and the inner layer—the dermis—is made up of tougher tissue fibers, among them collagen.

Any sort of significant damage to these skin layers can be life threatening. The World Health Organization estimates that more than 320,000 deaths occur worldwide each year due to skin injuries, particularly burns from fires. Many other burn victims survive but must thereafter live with pain and disfigurement unless doctors can intervene and rebuild some of their damaged skin.

One of the standard ways of rebuilding damaged skin has long been applying skin grafts. Thin slices of skin from undamaged sections of a patient's body, the grafts are sutured (or sometimes stapled) to the injured areas. Another grafting technique utilizes skin taken from cadavers (dead bodies). That approach is less successful though because the recipient's body tends to reject transplanted tissues.

The 1980s witnessed a major advance when researchers discovered how to grow new skin from special cells taken from the patient. Those cells, called fibroblasts, are the most common ones in the connective tissue of animals and humans. (Connective tissue consists of masses of tough, sturdy cells that bind other kinds of tissues—such as muscle and nerve tissues—to one another.) First, the researchers constructed a scaffolding, which is a network of tough fibers on which to grow the new cells. Then they affixed some fibroblasts to the scaffolding, and the attached cells began to multiply. Once a sufficient mass of new cells had grown, it was grafted onto the damaged skin area.

fibroblasts

the most common cells in the connective tissue of animals and humans

Higher Quality and Faster Growth

During the first few years of the twenty-first century, scientists who had been working for a while in the relatively new science

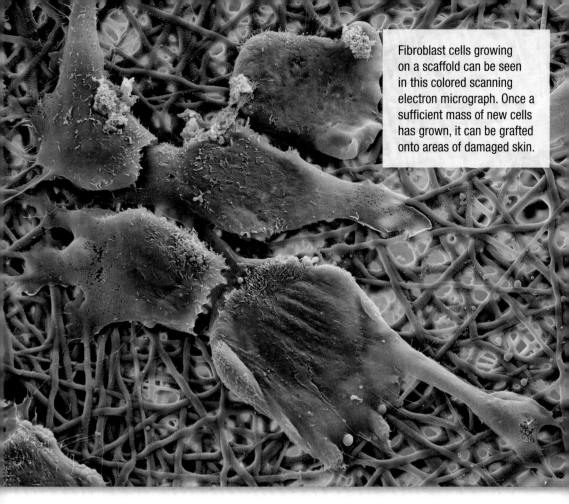

Fibroblast cells growing on a scaffold can be seen in this colored scanning electron micrograph. Once a sufficient mass of new cells has grown, it can be grafted onto areas of damaged skin.

of nanotechnology made a crucial observation. They recognized that the standard methods of repairing damaged skin could be significantly improved and expanded by adding nanomaterials to the mix. "It was the beginning of an entirely new scientific field, somewhere between medicine and nanotechnology,"[59] says Johannes Heitz, a scientist at the University of Linz in Austria.

One way that the use of nanomaterials improved the process of growing new skin was to provide more regularity and consistency on a nanoscale. In the standard tissue-growing method, it is typical for some of the cells to develop erratically. As a result, there are usually many random imperfections in the newly grown patch of skin. In contrast, the new method uses a scaffold made

scaffold

in the discipline of nanotechnology, a network of tough fibers on which technicians grow new cells of a special polymer, a synthetic chemical similar to nylon and acrylic. The polymer's repeating structures are on a nanoscale—each measuring from ten to twenty nanometers across—and are extremely regular. In fact, that "regular structure is essential if the material is to be used for the purpose of growing human cells,"[60] remarks Henryk Fiederowicz of the Military University of Technology in Warsaw, Poland. Moreover, he says, researchers have found that nanoscale polymers not only create a higher-quality patch of new skin but also grow tissue faster than traditional techniques.

Another advantage of using nanoscale structures to grow new skin relates to the adhesion, or sticking ability, of the new tissue to the area of damaged tissue. "One of the main difficulties found in the application of this artificial skin is the problem [of] adhesion,"[61] states Macarena Perán of Spain's University of Jaen. To solve this problem, Perán and other experts are using the process of electrospinning to construct nanoscale scaffolds. The process starts with a tiny droplet containing collagen fibers similar to those in the skin's dermis. When a thin needle carrying an electric current touches the droplet, a supermicroscopic stream of nanofibers shoots outward. The fibers settle into a membrane that mimics the fibrous membranes in the skin and helps the new patch of grown skin adhere to the wound area.

Closing Wounds and Repairing Hearts

Nanomaterials have proven effective in binding together damaged tissues in a different way as well. Scientists in the United States and elsewhere are using gold nanoparticles to patch holes in blood vessels, skin, cartilage, intestines, and other organs. Before this development, surgeons had sometimes used the strong, highly focused light from a laser to fix such holes. The powerful laser light causes proteins in the surrounding tissues to fuse, thereby closing the wound.

One drawback of laser tissue welding, however, is that the welds are sometimes too weak and can reopen days, weeks, or months later. To solve this problem, researchers created a sort of glue made up of a composite of proteins and gold nanoparticles measuring approximately fifteen nanometers in diameter. Near-infrared light from a laser causes the glue to coagulate (clot or set), which closes the wound. The technique is in clinical trials and is expected to go into wide use in hospitals by the early 2020s.

Among the most dangerous holes and wounds that can appear in the body's tissues are those that occur in the walls of the four heart valves. Weakened valve walls and actual tears in those walls are immediately life threatening and often lead to heart attacks and death. Traditionally, surgeons operate and attempt to replace the defective tissues with human-made mechanical valves or patches of tissue grown with cells taken from the patient.

Nanotechnology has begun to offer alternatives to those standard methods. The primary strategy is tissue engineering to repair a heart valve or produce a fully functional new one. So far, lab experiments have produced new tissue patches grown on

Sunscreen, Lotion, and Nanotechnology

Scientific labs and companies around the world have paid tens of millions of dollars in recent years to fund research into ways to use nanotechnology to grow new skin for burn victims. That monetary investment pales in comparison, however, with the amounts the big cosmetic companies are pouring into nanotech research. Experts estimate that the over-the-counter skin care market, which includes skin creams and sunscreens, is worth some $12 billion per year. Moreover, the amount the cosmetics companies spend on nanotechnology research is steadily increasing with each passing year. This is because new sunscreens and lotions containing nanoparticles are generally superior to traditional versions. Older sunscreens have long employed ground-up macroparticles of iron, titanium, and zinc to help block ultraviolet light, which causes skin damage, including sunburns. (The term *macroparticle* refers to particles larger than nanoparticles, which are smaller than one hundred nanometers in width.) Those macroparticles need to be in greasy solutions and often produce certain unwanted results, such as irritating the skin or leaving a chalky residue on it. In contrast, sunscreens made with zinc and titanium nanoparticles easily dissolve in water-based topical preparations. Thus, they leave no film or residue on the skin and are less irritating than traditional sunscreens. Moreover, the nanoparticles are smaller than the wavelength of visible light and do a better job of blocking ultraviolet light.

scaffolds made of nanomaterials, similar to how new skin has been grown for burn victims. Scientists have implanted partial or full heart valves made this way into animals with a fair degree of success. After a while, their bodies absorbed the patches of cells grown on scaffolds and replaced them with normal tissues. According to Perán,

> Nano-engineered heart valves are a promising approach to overcome the limitations of conventional heart valve [replacements]. In fact, these valves have been tested in animal models showing excellent tissue remodeling. For instance, [heart cells grown on scaffolds] were inserted in a sheep model and, after three months, the [scaffold] was replaced by new tissue containing mature collagen along with functional blood vessels.[62]

A bioprinted tissue scaffold, created through a technique known as electrospinning, can be used to produce tissue patches for use in repairing heart valves and other organs—or for creating new, working organs.

Perán describes another successful example of an engineered heart valve that employed the electrospinning technique to aid in growing the new cells. The valve was implanted in the heart of a growing lamb. After eight months, the scaffold was totally absorbed and replaced by normal, healthy heart tissue.

Regenerating Lost Bone Tissue

Perán and other experts point out that perfecting this new approach to patching human hearts will require a number of clinical human trials and is therefore still a few years away. Yet she adds that "the data produced so far by the animal studies is extremely encouraging."[63] The same is true for the numerous medical studies presently looking into using nanomaterials to regenerate bone tissues affected by diseases such as osteoporosis. A destructive thinning of the bones, osteoporosis is caused by factors like advancing age, alcoholism, and particularly a diet deficient in calcium and vitamin D. Over time, the bone tissues become more porous and brittle.

The most common traditional treatment for osteoporosis is for the patient to consume large amounts of calcium supplements. These can slow down bone tissue loss and increase bone density to some degree. This approach has its disadvantages, however. Indian scientist Ayushi Shukla, who has experimented with nanoparticles to reverse bone loss, explains that taking large quantities of calcium supplements "has some side effects like constipation and increased incidence of cardiac diseases and stroke."[64]

Shukla and other researchers have so far explored two general approaches to using nanoparticles to regenerate thinning bone tissues. The first is to deliver to those tissues various chemicals that stimulate bone growth. To achieve this goal, scientists attach molecules of the chemicals to the surfaces of nanoparticles that have been magnetized. Then, using a strong magnetic field, they guide the particles into the affected bone tissues. The particles' magnetic properties have no harmful effect on the patient because, as Shukla says, they "lose their magnetism once the external magnetic field is removed."[65]

The other common approach to regenerating thinning bones through nanotechnology is to construct grafts of strong new bone and introduce them into the weakest areas of the bones. As in the case of growing skin grafts, medical experts create a scaffold on which to grow the new tissue. They have tried a number of different materials to construct these scaffolds, including chitin. A component of cell walls in animals, and in the hard exoskeletons of insects, crabs, and lobsters, chitin is biodegradable. That means that once it is introduced into the bone tissue, it will slowly break down and become a part of that tissue, hopefully strengthening it. Chitin is also porous on a nanoscale—that is, like bone, it features pores smaller than one hundred nanometers in diameter. For these and other reasons, chitin is being used more often in bone tissue engineering.

chitin

a component of cell walls in animals, and in the hard exoskeletons of insects, crabs, and lobsters

This and similar bone tissue regeneration techniques have shown repeated success in tests on rabbits and other lab animals. Clinical trials to test those promising new methods on human subjects are the next step on the path to regular application on patients in hospitals around the globe. For scientists like Shukla, who work on the front lines of the new research, that goal is vital because it will eventually save many lives:

> It is imperative to bring nanotechnology-based [techniques and medicines] from the laboratory into large scale manufacturing and conduct clinical trials for the same so that they can be put to use as quickly as possible. Nanotechnology provides abundant advantages and benefits which must be exploited for the betterment of humankind.[66]

Will Diseases Be a Thing of the Past?

Skin, heart, and bone tissues will not be the only masses of human body cells that will someday be routinely regenerated with the aid of nanotechnology, experts say. In the bright medical future that they foresee, the most delicate bodily tissues of all will also benefit from the use of nanomaterials. The tissues in question are those of the nerves and brain.

One area of research already under way focuses on the destructive effects of strokes and brain infections. In a stroke, blood is blocked from entering part of the brain, causing local brain cells to die. A brain infection, which occurs when germs invade brain tissue, can also kill brain cells. When groups of brain cells die, electrical signals can no longer pass through them. If they are large enough, these gaps in otherwise healthy brain tissue can seriously disrupt a person's ability to reason, understand, and remember.

Some scientists are addressing this problem by experimenting with carbon nanotubes. The idea is to take advantage of those particles' ability to conduct electrical pulses. The hope is that ways will be found to use the tiny tubes to carry electrical signals across the gaps formed by dead brain cells.

Scientists are exploring the use of chitin for repairing weak or damaged bone tissue. Chitin is a component found in the cell walls of crabs and other creatures with hard outer exoskeletons.

A bit further in the future than that achievement, some researchers predict, doctors will be able to implant miniature electrical circuits in place of the dead cells. In theory, that could restore a damaged brain to full function, eliminating the effects of strokes and brain infections. From that point, doctors will be only a step away from using nanotechnology for a much larger range of treatments for brain-related ailments. These might include therapies for depression, anxiety, and even personality disorders.

Some medical experts suggest that by the time doctors can overcome such brain-related disorders, most or even all traditional diseases will be a thing of the past. At least in part, they say, that amazing accomplishment will be an outgrowth of the nanotechnology revolution. As Perán puts it, "The advanced applications of [nanotechnology to] medicine will undoubtedly transform the fundamentals of diagnosis, treatment, and prevention of diseases, becoming an inevitable part of our life."[67]

Noted American computer scientist, inventor, and futurist Ray Kurzweil is convinced that such a miraculous-sounding medical

Not Simply a Pipe Dream

The idea of implanting nanocomputers in people's brains to allow them to merge with the Internet and eliminate most or all diseases in the process is not simply a pipe dream suggested by futurist Ray Kurzweil. The owners of many major companies agree that this idea is feasible and are already gearing up to make it a reality. Among those far-thinking corporate leaders is Elon Musk, the chief executive officer (CEO) of the major technology companies SpaceX and Tesla. Musk has given the green light to the development of a brain-computer link called Neuralink. He hopes that the implants will eventually lead to better-informed people who employ the technology in part to eliminate most or all diseases. Although such advanced implants still lie in the future, much simpler versions of them *have* been used by doctors for years. For example, arrays of electrodes and other similar devices have been used to help lessen the adverse effects of epilepsy, Parkinson's, and other diseases that affect the brain and nerves. Another wealthy corporate CEO, entrepreneur Bryan Johnson, wants to create advanced versions of such implants to eventually eradicate, or at least totally control, epilepsy and similar illnesses. In 2013 Johnson founded Kernel, the company that will manufacture the advanced implants, which will take advantage of the latest discoveries in nanotechnology.

future will become a reality within a mere few decades. Moreover, he says, it will be possible not only to repair brain, nerve, and other tissues but also to enhance their normal structure and abilities. This will happen, Kurzweil foretells, when nanocomputer systems, partly assembled by tiny nanorobots, are implanted in the body.

To Replicate Intelligence
Implanting such systems in the brain will have especially life-altering consequences, Kurzweil predicts. In a very real sense, this will be equivalent to having an advanced cell phone that exists within the brain tissues and melds with one's mind. On the one hand, the person's brain will be able to directly connect to the so-called cloud (the term for the Internet's collective storage facilities). On the other, the person will be able to communicate, in a sort of telepathy, with anyone else in the world whose brain has been enhanced in the same manner.

This is sure to begin changing the very nature of what people have long perceived as reality. In Kurzweil's words, "we are about to see a revolution emerge in virtual and augmented reality."[68] That radical change in the human condition, he adds, will be motivated by a yearning even stronger than the desire of doctors to heal. Humanity will be transformed, he insists, by the driving urge to replicate intelligence itself, the "most important and powerful attribute of human civilization."[69]

SOURCE NOTES

Introduction: The Incredibly Tiny Nano Realm

1. Sam Wong, "New Nanotech Weapons Could Reduce Deaths from Bacterial Infections," Imperial College London, September 7, 2012. www3.imperial.ac.uk.
2. Quoted in Wong, "New Nanotech Weapons Could Reduce Deaths from Bacterial Infections."
3. Wong, "New Nanotech Weapons Could Reduce Deaths from Bacterial Infections."
4. Center for Responsible Nanotechnology, "What Is Nanotechnology?" www.crnanao.org.
5. Quoted in Morgan O'Rourke, "Smaller and Smaller and Smaller: Examining the Possibilities of Nanotechnology," Risk Management Society. http://cf.rims.org.
6. Quoted in Olga Oksman, "How Nanotechnology Research Could Cure Cancer and Other Diseases," *Guardian* (Manchester), June 11, 2016. www.theguardian.com.
7. Linda Williams and Wade Adams, *Nanotechnology Demystified*. New York: McGraw-Hill, 2007, pp. 17–18.

Chapter 1: The Origins of Nanotechnology

8. Michio Kaku, *Physics of the Future*. New York: Doubleday, 2011, p. 200.
9. Richard P. Feynman, "There's Plenty of Room at the Bottom," Nanotechnology. www.zyvex.com/nano.
10. Feynman, "There's Plenty of Room at the Bottom."
11. Feynman, "There's Plenty of Room at the Bottom."
12. Kaku, *Physics of the Future*, p. 178.
13. Quoted in Priya Ganapati, "20 Years of Moving Atoms, One by One," *Wired*, September 30, 2009. www.wired.com.
14. Williams and Adams, *Nanotechnology Demystified*, p. 13.
15. Quoted in Monica Heger, "A Silver Coating in the Fight Against Microbes," *Scientific American*, May 2, 2008. www.scientificamerican.com.

16. K. Eric Drexler, *Engines of Creation: The Coming Era of Nanotechnology*. New York: Anchor, 1986, p. 63.
17. K. Eric Drexler, *Radical Abundance: How a Revolution in Nanotechnology Will Change Civilization*. New York: PublicAffairs, 2013, pp. 284, 286.

Chapter 2: Nanotechnology and Medical Diagnosis

18. Quoted in James McIntosh, "Nanosensors: The Future of Diagnostic Medicine?," Medical News Today, January 14, 2016. www.medicalnewstoday.com.
19. Quoted in McIntosh, "Nanosensors."
20. R.K. Satvokar et al., "Emerging Trends in Medical Diagnosis: A Thrust on Nanotechnology," *Medicinal Chemistry*, OMICS International. www.omicsonline.org.
21. Quoted in Phys.org, "Better Contrast Agents Based on Nanoparticles," August 3, 2016. https://phys.org.
22. Quoted in McIntosh, "Nanosensors."
23. Quoted in McIntosh, "Nanosensors."
24. Quoted in McIntosh, "Nanosensors."
25. McIntosh, "Nanosensors."
26. Quoted in University of Georgia, "Gold Nanoparticles Used to Diagnose Flu in Minutes," ScienceDaily, August 4, 2011. www.sciencedaily.com.
27. Quoted in University of Georgia, "Gold Nanoparticles Used to Diagnose Flu in Minutes."
28. Quoted in Todd B. Bates, "Graphene-Based Sensor Could Improve Evaluation, Diagnosis, and Treatment of Asthma," Rutgers Today, May 22, 2017. http://news.rutgers.edu.
29. Williams and Adams, *Nanotechnology Demystified*, p. 93.
30. Williams and Adams, *Nanotechnology Demystified*, p. 95.

Chapter 3: Nanoscale Delivery of Medicines

31. Varun Arora, "Nanotechnology Drug Delivery Systems: An Insight," *CureTalk* (blog), Trialx, October 17, 2012. http://trialx .com.
32. Quoted in Earl Boysen and Nancy Boysen, "Researchers Develop Sticky Nanoparticles to Fight Heart Disease," Understanding Nanotechnology. www.understandingnano.com.
33. Quoted in Boysen and Boysen, "Researchers Develop Sticky Nanoparticles to Fight Heart Disease."

34. Earl Boysen and Nancy Boysen, "Injectable Nano-Network Controls Blood Sugar in Diabetics for Days at a Time," Understanding Nanotechnology. www.understandingnano.com.
35. Quoted in Boysen and Boysen, "Injectable Nano-Network Controls Blood Sugar in Diabetics for Days at a Time."
36. Josh Martinez, "Is the Nanopatch the Future of Vaccines?," Passport Health, June 29, 2017. www.passporthealthusa.com.
37. K.H. Hassan Reza et al., "Nanorobots: The Future Trend of Drug Delivery and Therapeutics," *International Journal of Pharmaceutical Sciences Review and Research*, vol. 10, September/October 2011, p. 65.
38. Reza et al., "Nanorobots," p. 62.

Chapter 4: Curing Cancer

39. National Cancer Institute, "What Is Cancer?" www.cancer.gov.
40. Krista Conger, "How Nanotechnology Could Detect and Treat Cancer," Phys.org, May 18, 2016. https://phys.org.
41. Quoted in Conger, "How Nanotechnology Could Detect and Treat Cancer."
42. Quoted in Conger, "How Nanotechnology Could Detect and Treat Cancer."
43. Quoted in Conger, "How Nanotechnology Could Detect and Treat Cancer."
44. Conger, "How Nanotechnology Could Detect and Treat Cancer."
45. Quoted in Conger, "How Nanotechnology Could Detect and Treat Cancer."
46. Sanjiv Sam Gambhir, "Nanotechnology in Cancer Imaging," NCI Alliance for Nanotechnology in Cancer, December 17, 2010, podcast. https://nano.cancer.gov.
47. Quoted in Conger, "How Nanotechnology Could Detect and Treat Cancer."
48. Quoted in Leigh Krietsch Boerner, "Nanoparticles Show Big Promise in the Fight Against Cancer," *Nova Next*, July 2, 2013. www.pbs.org.
49. Quoted in Phys.org, "Shape-Shifting Engineered Nanoparticles for Delivering Cancer Drugs to Tumors," February 19, 2016. https://phys.org.

50. Quoted in Phys.org, "Shape-Shifting Engineered Nanoparticles for Delivering Cancer Drugs to Tumors."
51. Quoted in Phys.org, "Shape-Shifting Engineered Nanoparticles for Delivering Cancer Drugs to Tumors."
52. Quoted in Earl Boysen and Nancy Boysen, "Nanoparticles Combine Photodynamic and Molecular Therapies Against Pancreatic Cancer," Understanding Nanotechnology. www.understandingnano.com.
53. Quoted in Earl Boysen and Nancy Boysen, "New System Uses Nanodiamonds to Deliver Chemotherapy Drugs Directly to Brain Tumors," Understanding Nanotechnology. www.understandingnano.com.
54. Quoted in Alison E. Berman, "How Nanotech Will Lead to a Better Future for Us All," Singularity Hub, August 12, 2016. https://singularityhub.com.
55. Quoted in Berman, "How Nanotech Will Lead to a Better Future for Us All."
56. Avnesh S. Thakor and Sanjiv S. Gambhir, "Nanooncology: The Future of Cancer Diagnosis and Therapy," Wiley Online Library. http://onlinelibrary.wiley.com.
57. Thakor and Gambhir, "Nanooncology."

Chapter 5: Nanoparticles Rebuild Bodily Tissues

58. Quoted in Berman, "How Nanotech Will Lead to a Better Future for Us All."
59. Quoted in Eureka, "Nanotech Medicine to Rebuild Damaged Parts of Human Body," ScienceDaily, January 19, 2011. www.sciencedaily.com.
60. Quoted in Eureka, "Nanotech Medicine to Rebuild Damaged Parts of Human Body."
61. Macarena Perán et al., "How Can Nanotechnology Help to Repair the Body? Advances in Cardiac, Skin, Bone, Cartilage and Nerve Tissue Regeneration," *Materials*, vol. 6, no. 4, 2013. www.mdpi.com.
62. Perán et al., "How Can Nanotechnology Help to Repair the Body?"
63. Perán et al., "How Can Nanotechnology Help to Repair the Body?"

64. Ayushi Shukla et al., "Nanotechnology Towards Prevention of Anaemia and Osteoporosis: From Concept to Market," Taylor & Francis Online. www.tandfonline.com.

65. Shukla et al., "Nanotechnology Towards Prevention of Anaemia and Osteoporosis."

66. Shukla et al., "Nanotechnology Towards Prevention of Anaemia and Osteoporosis."

67. Perán et al., "How Can Nanotechnology Help to Repair the Body?"

68. Quoted in Brian Buntz, "Optimistic Projections Regarding the Future of Nanotechnology," *MPMN Medtech Pulse* (blog), February 18, 2016. www.qmed.com.

69. Quoted in Sveta McShane and Jason Dorrier, "Ray Kurzweil Predicts Three Technologies Will Define Our Future," Singularity Hub, April 19, 2016. https://singularityhub.com.

FOR FURTHER RESEARCH

Books
John Allen, *What Is the Future of Nanotechnology?* San Diego: ReferencePoint, 2017.

Lisa J. Amstutz, *Discover Nanotechnology*. Minneapolis: Lerner, 2016.

David Filmore, *Nanobots for Dinner: Preparing for the Technological Singularity*. Charleston: Create Space, 2016.

Marty Gitlin, *Nanomedicine*. North Mankato, MN: Cherry Lake, 2017.

Chakrapani Srinivase, *Know About Nanotechnology*. Seattle: Amazon Digital Services, 2016.

Steven Vetter, *Of Several Worlds: A Post-Nanotechnology Adventure*. Seattle: Amazon Digital Services, 2016.

Internet Sources
Alison E. Berman, "How Nanotech Will Lead to a Better Future for Us All," Singularity Hub, August 12, 2016. https://singularityhub.com/2016/08/12/how-nanotech-will-lead-to-a-better-future-for-us-all.

Brian Buntz, "Self-Healing Bone Thanks to Nanoshells," *MPMN Medtech Pulse* (blog), February 18, 2016. www.qmed.com/mpmn/medtechpulse/self-healing-bone-thanks-nanoshells.

Teresa Matich, "Nanotechnology in Medicine," Investing News Network, August 9, 2016. http://investingnews.com/daily/tech-investing/nanotech-investing/nanotechnology-in-medicine.

Sveta McShane and Jason Dorrier, "Ray Kurzweil Predicts Three Technologies Will Define Our Future," Singularity Hub, April 19, 2016. https://singularityhub.com/2016/04/19/ray-kurzweil-predicts-three-technologies-will-define-our-future.

Qmed Staff, "10 Nanotech Breakthroughs You Should Know About (Updated)," Qmed. www.qmed.com/mpmn/article/10 -nanotech-breakthroughs-you-should-know-about-updated.

Kristopher Sturgis, "Delving Into the Secrets of Nanoparticles," *MPMN Medtech Pulse* (blog), May 3, 2016. www.qmed.com /mpmn/medtechpulse/delving-secrets-nanoparticles.

Websites

Nanowerk (www.nanowerk.com). This useful, easy-to-read on-line site provides all sorts of information about nanotechnology. It has general information as well as articles that describe the latest work in medicine and other fields of study.

Science for the Public (www.scienceforthepublic.org). This on-line science network includes a section titled "Breakthroughs in Nanotechnology," which provides links to various articles about recent discoveries related to the use of nanotechnology for medical diagnosis.

Understanding Nanotechnology (www.understandingnano.com). This excellent website is maintained by engineer Earl Boysen and his wife, writer Nancy Boysen. It explains the concept of nanoscale drug delivery in fairly simple terms and provides handy links to several supporting articles about ongoing studies.

INDEX

PICTURE CREDITS

In addition to his numerous acclaimed volumes on ancient civilizations, historian Don Nardo has published several studies of scientific discoveries and phenomena, including *Deadliest Dinosaurs*, *Climate Change*, *Polar Explorations*, *Volcanoes*, *Science and Sustainable Energy*, and award-winning books on astronomy and space exploration. Mr. Nardo also composes and arranges orchestral music. He lives with his wife, Christine, in Massachusetts.